A CASE STUDY OF PALLIKARANAI MARSHLAND

WETLANDS

Environmental Degradation, Water Quality and Economic Valuation of Wetlands

Jayanthi Murali

Notion Press

No. 8, 3rd Cross Street
CIT Colony, Mylapore
Chennai, Tamil Nadu – 600004

First Published by Notion Press 2021
Copyright © Jayanthi Murali 2021
All Rights Reserved.

ISBN 978-1-64983-716-5

ACKNOWLEDGMENT

Writing a book about a topic that is close to my heart is a surreal process and I'm forever indebted to and must acknowledge several people who have supported, influenced, and inspired me to successfully complete this work.

First and foremost, I am grateful to my mentor, **Dr. P. Duraisamy**, for his valuable guidance, encouragement, expertise, and inspiration. With a deep sense of gratitude, I wish to express my sincere thanks to **Professor Krishan Kant Sharma, Dr. A. Ramachandran, Dr. L. Venkatachalam, Dr. K. S. Kavi Kumar, Dr. Jayashree Vencatesan,** and **Thiru. R. Rajasekhar, NEER Trust,** for their valuable contribution of expertise and knowledge sharing throughout my work.

My sincere thanks to colleagues and friends from the **Tamil Nadu Forests Department, Environment Department, Government of Tamil Nadu** for helping to turn my ideas into stories. My special thanks to Dr. R. Prasannavenkatesh and S. Lakshmi Sundaram for their help in revising the manuscript in the book format.

My deepest thanks from the bottom of my heart to all the members of my family, especially **my mother, my parents-in-law, my brother,** and **his family**. My special gratitude goes to my husband, **Dr. Jayanth Murali, I. P. S.,** and my daughters **Anisha** and **Anussha** who are my greatest inspiration and who light up my life every single day with their never-ending love and encouraging ways.

Last, but definitely not least, I thank **my father**, who has passed away years ago. His unwavering support in my education has made me reach this stage of my life. For all those whose names do not find a mention here but have helped me, I am filled with deep gratitude for them.

– Jayanthi Murali

PREAMBLE

Wetlands function as natural sponges, which are vital parts of the hydrological cycle. They are highly productive and support exceptionally large biological diversity, which provides a wide range of ecosystem services and socio-economic benefits, such as food and fiber, waste assimilation, water purification, flood mitigation, erosion control, groundwater recharge, microclimate regulation, enhancing the aesthetic of the landscape, supporting many significant recreational, social, and cultural activities in addition to being a part of our cultural heritage.

In this context, this book will act as a ready reckoner for policy managers for framing suitable management practices that will help to revive and rejuvenate the existing wetlands in the plight of climate change. In particular, the wetlands will act as a carbon sink for natural sequestration. Enhancing wetlands will help to meet the sustainable development goals and focus on aquatic ecosystem conservation, restoration, and management, including the hydrological and the biophysical aspects. It is highly warranted that community participation is the key player in conserving natural resources.

This book compiles the microscopic research of environmental degradation, threats, related key issues, and changes in land use with respect to the Pallikaranai Marsh. This book also deals with water quality issues and socio-economic aspects of the urban wetlands through the public/community participatory approach.

MOTIVATION

Wetlands are considered the most biologically diverse of all ecosystems, serving as a home to a wide range of plant and animal life. Society as a stakeholder should shoulder responsibilities to cope up with environmental change. A healthy environment is the need of the hour, not a healthy economy, as nature provides enough to quench the need of the ecosystem not the greed of the individual. Therefore, protection of the environment is often a matter of contention.

Protection of wetlands is based on the premise that preservation of a specific ecosystem type can be of sufficient common interest that its conversion or development should be prevented or restrained by law. To some, the universal protection of wetlands seems an infringement of property rights. To others, it is a reasonable extension of the need. This all serves as the fuel to ignite the thoughts of the author.

Jayanthi Murali *with the love and soulful interest toward conserving nature drove the research on conserving the urban wetlands, considering the ecological aspect, which is the motive behind the birth of this book. She is the present Additional Principal Chief Conservator of Forest and the Secretary, Tamil Nadu Biodiversity Board.*

CONTENTS

LIST OF FIGURES

LIST OF TABLES

ABBREVIATIONS

$	-	Dollar
Al	-	Aluminum
APHA	-	American Public Health Association
ASCR	-	Automatic Scatter Gram Controlled Regression
Ba	-	Barium
BDL	-	Below detectable limit
Bo	-	Boron
BOD	-	Biological Oxygen Demand
BPO	-	Business process outsourcing
Ca	-	Calcium
CCC&AR	-	Centre for Climate Change And Adaptation Research
CCRCP	-	Chennai City River Conservation Project
Cd	-	Cadmium
CGWB	-	Central Ground Water Board
CMWSSB	-	Chennai Metro Water and Sewerage Supply Board
CNY	-	Yuan (Chinese Currency)
Co	-	Cobalt
COD	-	Chemical Oxygen Demand
CPCB	-	Central Pollution Central Board
CPHEEO	-	Central Public Health and Environmental Engineering Organisation
Cr	-	Chromium
Cu	-	Copper
CVM	-	Contingent Valuation Method
CWET	-	Central Wind Energy Technology
DC	-	Dichotomous Choice

DO	-	Dissolved Oxygen
EC	-	Electrical Conductivity
EMP	-	Environment Management Plan
ENVI	-	Environment for Visualizing Images
ETM	-	Enhanced Thematic Mapper
Fe	-	Iron
GIS	-	Geographical Information Systems
GOI	-	Government of India
GPS	-	Global Positioning System
INR	-	Indian Rupee (Rs)
IRS	-	Institute of Remote Sensing
ISRO	-	Indian Space Research Organisation
IT	-	Information Technology
ITES	-	Information Technology Enabled Services
IUCN	-	International Union for Conservation of Nature
K	-	Potassium
Km	-	Kilometer
LULCC	-	Land Use land Cover Changes
M/F	-	Male/Female
Mg	-	Magnesium
mg/l	-	Milligrams per Liter
MLD	-	Million Liters per day
Mn	-	Manganese
MoEF&CC	-	Ministry of Environment, Forest and Climate Change
MRTS	-	Mass Rapid Transit System
MSS	-	Multi-spectral Scanner
MSWM	-	Municipal Solid Waste Management
MT	-	Metric Ton
NGO	-	Non-Government Organization
Ni	-	Nickel
NIOT	-	National Institute of Ocean Technology
NOAA	-	National Oceanic and Atmospheric Administration
NWTP	-	Not Willing to Pay
OE	-	Open-ended

Pb	-	Lead
PC	-	Payment Card
pH	-	Potential Hydrogen (Hydrogen ion concentration)
PVC	-	Poly Vinyl Chloride
PWD	-	Public Works Department
RDBMS	-	Relational Database Management Systems
RP model	-	Revealed Preference Model
RS	-	Remote Sensing
Rs	-	Rupees
S	-	Sulfur
SAC	-	Space Applications Centre
SACON	-	Sálim Ali Centre for Ornithology and Natural History
SP model	-	Stated Preference Method
Sr	-	Strontium
SRMs	-	Standard Reference Materials
STP	-	Sewage Treatment Plant
TCLP	-	Toxicity Characteristics Leaching Procedure
TCM	-	Travel Cost Method
TDS	-	Total Dissolved Solids
TEV	-	Total Economic Valuation
TH	-	Total Hardness
TM	-	Thematic Mapper
TNPCB	-	Tamil Nadu Pollution Control Board
TSS	-	Total Soluble Salts
TTM	-	Total Trace Metals
TWAD	-	Tamil Nadu Water Supply and Drainage Board
UN	-	United Nations
UNEP	-	United Nations Environment Programme
USEPA	-	United States Environmental Protection Agency
UTM	-	Universal Traverse Mercator
VALSCL	-	Value Scale
WTA	-	Willingness To Accept
WTP	-	Willingness To Pay
Zn	-	Zinc

INTRODUCTION

Water has become a vital natural resource in the twenty-first century. In some countries, it may become the most critical issue influencing political and social events in the immediate future. India though enjoys a relatively moderate average-rainfall and experiences scarcity of water in many parts, resulting in the gradual development of this resource into a critical issue in the country. Most city authorities are unable to provide the required minimum water to their citizens. Even in areas with high rainfall, water scarcity is common during non-rainy months. *Water body* is a commonly used term to describe any place that holds water. The water bodies can be classified in many ways by their sizes, locations, water quality, aquatic ecology, and others. Important water bodies are the sea, rivers, ponds, lakes, and the wetlands; these may be artificial or natural, static or flowing, sweet or brackish, deep or shallow, permanent, or temporary. Environmentally, these water bodies serve the purpose of an open space in crowded urban localities. These water bodies have much ecological, social, religious, and economic importance. Thus, urban water bodies are a very special component in water use management to which, as of now, very little attention has been paid.

Wetlands are among the most productive life-supporting systems of the world with immense socio-economic, ecological, and bio-aesthetic importance. Wetlands provide diverse tangible and intangible benefits to humankind on a sustainable basis. Wetlands function like natural tubs or sponges, storing water and releasing it gradually. This process reduces flood heights and facilitates groundwater recharge, which contributes base flow to surface water systems during lean periods. The water storage capacity is noteworthy in reducing the chances of flooding. Hence, wetlands have been described both as *the kidneys of the landscape*, because of the functions they perform in the hydrological and chemical cycles, and also as *biological supermarkets*, because of the extensive food webs and rich biodiversity they support (Mitsch and Gosselink, 1993).

Wetland management, as the applied side of wetland science, requires an understanding of the scientific aspects of wetlands balanced with legal, institutional, and economic realities. As interest in wetlands has grown, so too have professional organizations and agencies that are concerned with wetlands as well as the number of journals and literature on wetland science.

Wetlands play major roles in the landscape by providing unique habitats for a wide variety of flora and fauna. Now that we have become concerned about the health of our entire planet, wetlands are being described by some as important carbon sinks and climate stabilizers on a global scale.

Wetlands have been and continue to be part of many human cultures in the world. Coles and Coles (1989) referred to the people who live in proximity to wetlands and whose culture is linked to them as Wet Landers. Most recently, wetlands have become the focus for eco-tourism in many developing and developed parts of the world. Scientists, engineers, lawyers, and regulators are now finding it both useful and necessary to become specialists in wetland ecology and wetland management in order to understand, preserve, and even reconstruct these fragile ecosystems.

TYPES OF WETLAND

In trying to categorize the wide range of wetlands encompassed by the Ramsar definition, Scott and Jones (1995) defined 30 groups of natural wetlands and nine man-made ones. However, for illustrative purposes, it is possible to identify five broad wetland systems:

- Estuaries – where rivers meet the sea and salinity is intermediate between salt and freshwater (e.g., deltas, mudflats, salt marshes).
- Marine – not influenced by river flows (e.g., shorelines and coral reefs).
- Riverine – land periodically inundated by river overtopping (e.g., water meadows, flooded forests, oxbow lakes).
- Palustrine – where there is more or less permanent water (e.g., papyrus swamp, marshes, and fen).
- Lacustrine – areas of permanent water with little flow (e.g., ponds, kettle lakes, volcanic crater lakes).

Wetland systems directly support millions of people and provide goods and services to the world outside the wetland. People use wetland soils for agriculture, they catch wetland fish to eat, and they cut wetland trees for timber and fuelwood and wetland reeds to make mats and thatched roofs. Direct use may also take the form of recreation, such as bird watching, sailing, or scientific study. Apart from using the wetlands directly, people indirectly benefit from wetland functions or services. As floodwater flows out over a floodplain wetland, the water is temporarily stored; this reduces the peak river level and delays the time of the peak, which can be a benefit to riparian dwellers downstream.

As mangroves recycle nitrogen, they improve water quality downstream. By benefiting in this way, people are making indirect use of the wetland functions. These functions may be performed by engineering schemes such as dams, sea walls, or water treatment plants, but such technological solutions are normally more expensive than when performed by wetlands.

Wetlands, worldwide, face a range of anthropogenic threats like the dumping of solid wastes, burning of garbage, and disposal of sewage water in and around wetlands. The chief indirect drivers of change are human population growth around wetlands coupled with growing economic and commercial activities. Major direct threats for wetlands are infrastructure development (dams, dykes, roads, residential and commercial buildings), land reclamation, and over-harvesting. Major indirect ones are aquaculture, agriculture, reduced water flow, depletion of ground and surface water supplies, introduction of invasive alien species, organic and inorganic pollutants-quantity and flow rate,increasing pollutant inputs,changing species composition as a result of disturbance and the introduction of non-invasive species.

WETLAND LOSS

Wetlands are dynamic systems, continually undergoing natural change due to subsidence, drought, sea level rise, or infilling with sediment or organic material. Thus, many wetlands are only temporary features of the landscape and will be expected to change and eventually disappear while new wetlands are created elsewhere. Direct and indirect human activity has considerably altered the rate of change in wetlands. To some degree, we have created new artificial wetlands by building reservoirs, canals, and flood storage areas. However, the loss of wetlands has far outstripped the gains.

The view that wetlands are wastelands, resulting from ignorance or misunderstanding of the value of the goods and services available, has led to their conversion for the purpose of intensive agricultural, industrial, or residential use. The individual desires of farmers or developers have been supported by government policy and subsidies. In addition to direct action on the land, river engineering schemes have diverted water away from wetlands, as it has been believed that this water is wasted in the wetland or at least has a lower value than its use for rice irrigation upstream. Some organizations still look upon wetlands only in terms of their potential to provide farmland to feed an ever-expanding population, which normally requires alteration of the natural system. Wetlands may also be lost by pollution, waste disposal, mining, or groundwater abstraction.

It is probably safe to assume that we are still losing wetlands at a fairly rapid rate globally and that we have perhaps lost as much as 50 percent of the original wetlands. There are a number of areas where the loss rate has been documented. The estimate of about 50 percent loss of wetlands since European settlement in the lower 48 percent in the United States of America is fairly accurate as is the 90 percent loss of wetlands in New Zealand.

STATUS OF WETLANDS

STATUS AND TRENDS OF WETLANDS AROUND THE GLOBE

Wetlands cover 6% of the world's land surface and contain about 12% of the global carbon pool, playing an important role in the global carbon cycle (Erwin, 2009). The global extent of wetlands is estimated to be 1,280 million hectares (1.2 million square kilometers) but it is well established that this is an underestimate. This estimate includes inland and coastal wetlands (including lakes, rivers, and marshes), near-shore marine areas (to a depth of 6 meters below low tide), and human-made wetlands such as reservoirs and rice fields and was derived from multiple information sources.

More than 50% of specific types of wetlands in parts of North America, Europe, Australia, and New Zealand were converted during the twentieth century. For North America, the estimates refer to inland water, coastal marshes, and emergent estuarine wetlands; the estimates for Europe include the loss of peatlands; those for Northern Australia are of freshwater marshes; while estimates for New Zealand are of inland and coastal marshes. There is insufficient information on the extent of all wetland types being considered in this report – such as inland wetlands that are seasonally or intermittently flooded and some coastal wetlands – to document the extent of wetland loss globally. There is, however, ample evidence of the dramatic loss and degradation of many individual wetlands (Davis, 1993).

Coastal ecosystems are among the most productive yet highly threatened systems in the world. These ecosystems produce disproportionately more services relating to human well-being than most other systems, even those covering larger total areas, but are experiencing some of the most rapid degradation and loss in mangroves and coral reefs (Millennium Ecosystem Assessment, 2005).

By way of comparison, a total of 1.2 million sq. km of wetlands has been registered with the Ramsar Convention on Wetlands of International Importance as of 2004. This represents about 13 to 17 percent of the world's total wetlands (Mitsch and Jorgensen, 2004).

WETLANDS OF INDIA

A survey by the Ministry of Environment, Forest and Climate Change in 1990 estimated that about 1.5 million hectares are under natural wetlands and that man-made wetlands like tanks and reservoirs occupy 2.6 million hectares. Most wetlands of India are directly or indirectly associated with the river systems. Being very rich in wetland resources, India exhibits significant ecological diversity, primarily because of variability in climatic conditions and changing topography. However, according to the Directory of Asian Wetlands, wetlands in India occupy some 58.2 million hectares and some 93 wetlands meet the criteria under the Ramsar Convention.

Wetlands in India are distributed in different geographical regions ranging from the Himalayas to the Deccan Plateau. The variability in climatic conditions and topography is responsible for significant diversity. They are classified into different types based on their origin, vegetation, nutrient status, and thermal characteristics (Pandey et al., 1997). This great diversity of wetlands supports an extremely rich biodiversity of flora and fauna. The various reservoirs, shallow ponds, and numerous tanks support wetland biodiversity and add to the country's wetland wealth. It is estimated that freshwater wetlands alone support 20 percent of the known range of biodiversity in India (Deepa and Ramachandra, 1999).

The natural lakes or wetlands of India may be considered separately for the three major geomorphic regions – the Himalayan region, the Ganga-Brahmaputra floodplain, Peninsular India. The salt lakes, coastal lagoons, and urban wetlands are included in these regions.

The oldest large urban wetland is the Upper Lake of Bhopal, which was constructed in the early 11th century. The Lower Lake of Bhopal was created much later as the city started sprawling on that side. Other old and well-known urban wetlands are those in Udaipur (Fateh Sagar, Pichola, Udai Sagar, and five other smaller lakes). Hyderabad (Hussain Sagar, Osman Sagar), Ajmer (Ana Sagar and Foy Sagar), Jaipur (Mansagar and Jamwa Ramgarh), Jodhpur (Sardar Samand), and Alwar (Siliserh). Similar lakes are common near many urban centers in Madhya Pradesh (e.g. Sagar, Rewa), Karnataka, and Gujarat. The recent man-made urban wetland Sukhna Lake near Chandigarh has attracted considerable attention due to the awful shrinkage rate and pollution. Some of the natural wetlands such as Dal Lake and Nainital Lake are also truly urban lakes (Gopal, 1996.). Similar stress should be given to the conservation of Pallikaranai Wetland in Chennai suburbs, the study location in the present study.

The *National Wetland Atlas*, prepared by the Space Applications Centre (SAC), ISRO, Ahmedabad, sponsored by the Ministry of

Environment, Forest and Climate Change (MoEF&CC), Govt. of India, in March 2011 revealed that the wetlands are classified into 19 classes. The natural wetlands that are the inland wetlands account for 43%, whereas the coastal wetlands account for 24%. (Figure 2.1) (National Wetland Atlas, 2011). Similarly, the type-wise wetland distribution in India is given in the Figure 2.2 from the *National Wetland Atlas* (2011). The graphic distribution of wetlands in the states shows that Tamil Nadu comes under the first ten states that have a greater area of wetlands (Figure 2.3) (National Wetland Atlas, 2011)

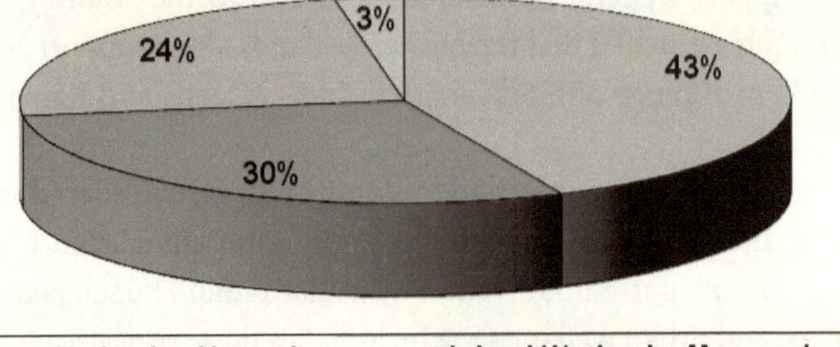

Source: National Wetland Atlas, 2011

▲ **Figure 2.1:**   Natural and Man-made Wetlands in India

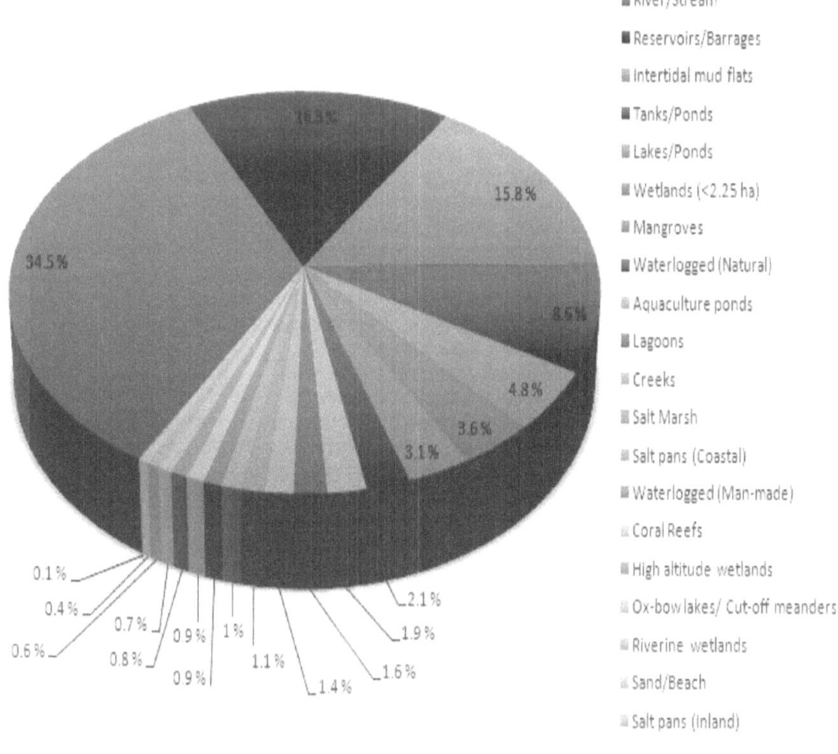

Source: National Wetland Atlas, 2011

▲ **Figure 2.2:**   Type-wise Wetland Distribution in India

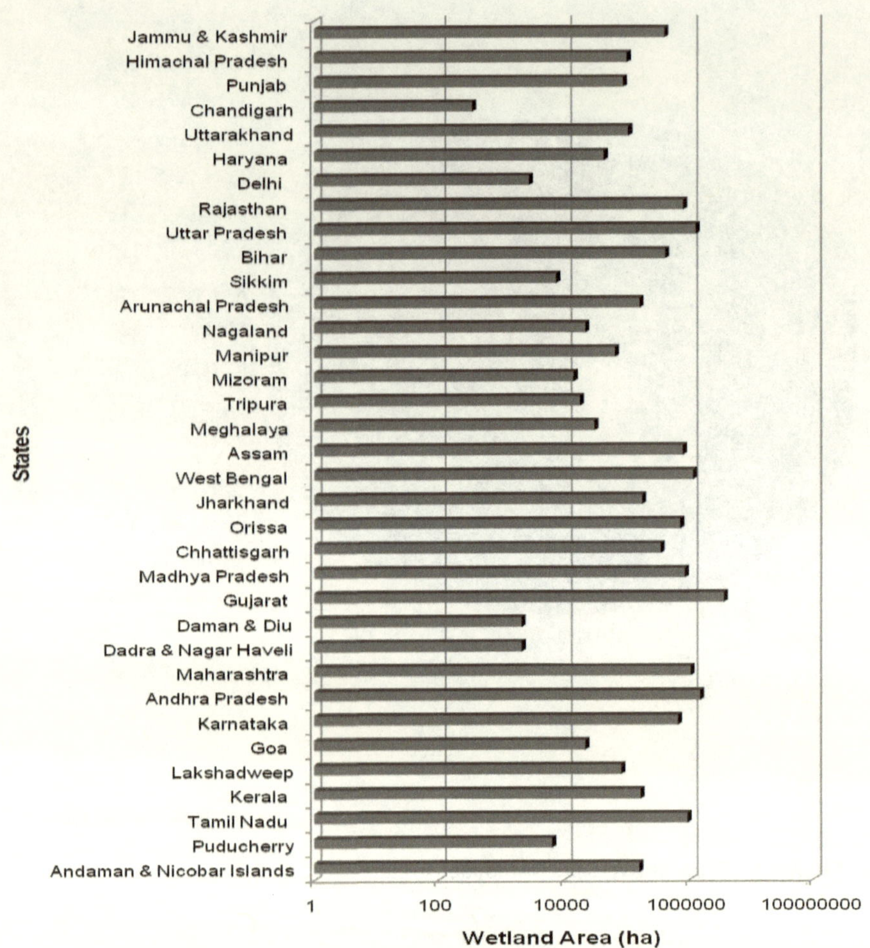

▲ **Figure 2.3:** State-wise Graphical Distribution of Wetlands in India

WETLANDS IN TAMIL NADU

In Tamil Nadu, the total wetland area estimated is 9,02,534 hectares, which is around 6.92 percent of the geographic area. The major wetland types are lake/pond (3,16,091 ha), tank/pond (2,37,613 ha), river/stream (1,36,878 ha), and reservoir/barrage (56,419 ha). The area under mangroves is around 7,315 ha. Coral reefs (3,899 ha) exist mainly in the

Ramanathapuram district. The wetlands occupy as high as 18.05 percent of the geographic area in Ramanathapuram and as low as 1.08 percent in Coimbatore. In terms of total wetland area, Kancheepuram is the leading district with 80,445 hectares (8.91%) and Chennai has the smallest area, 917 hectares (0.10%). While Ramanathapuram and Pudukkottai have over 70,000 hectares as the total wetland area, Sivaganga and Villupuram have over 60,000 hectares and Tiruvannamalai and Nagapattinam districts have a wetland area of over 50,000 hectares. (Figure 2.4) (National Wetland Atlas, 2011).

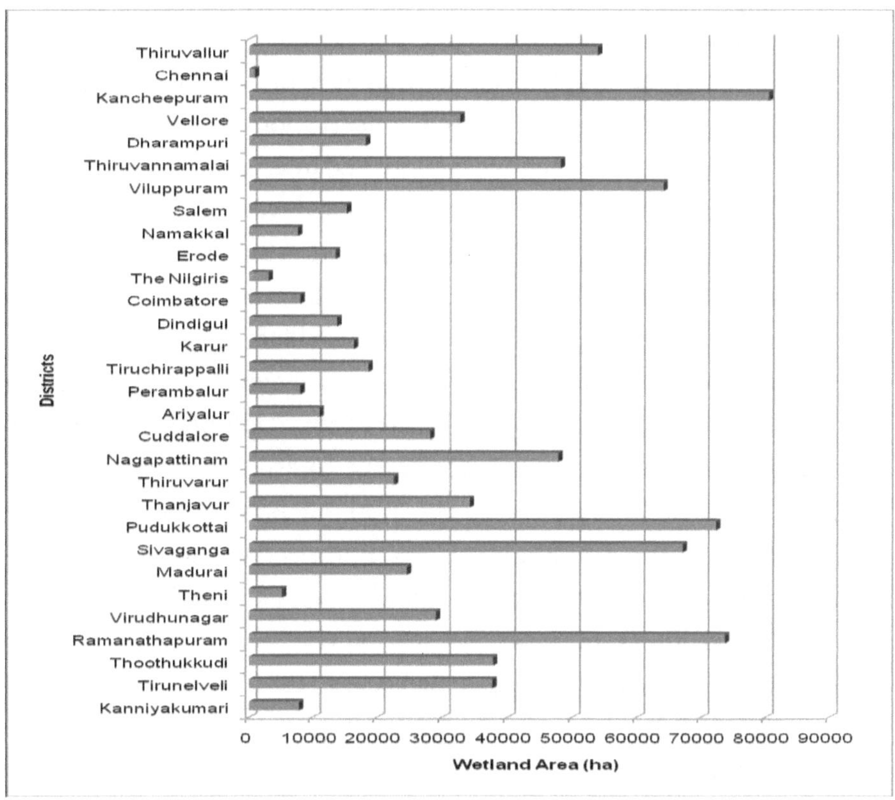

▲ **Figure 2.4:** District-wise Graphical Distribution of Wetlands in Tamil Nadu

Source: National Wetland Atlas, 2011

RAMSAR CONVENTION

The Convention on Wetlands of International Importance, called the Ramsar Convention, is an intergovernmental treaty that provides the framework for national action and international cooperation for the conservation and wise use of wetlands and their resources. Negotiated through the 1960s by countries and non-governmental organizations that were concerned at the increasing loss and degradation of wetland habitat for migratory waterbirds, the treaty was adopted in the Iranian city of Ramsar in 1971 and came into force in 1975. It is the only global environmental treaty that deals with a particular ecosystem, and the Convention's member countries cover all geographic regions of the planet.

The Convention's mission is "the conservation and wise use of all wetlands through local and national actions and international cooperation, as a contribution toward achieving sustainable development throughout the world." Therefore, *wise use* is the conservation and sustainable use of wetlands and their resources, for the benefit of humankind (Davis, 1993).

Support on wetland conservation is provided to the Convention from organizations such as the International Union for Conservation of Nature (IUCN), The World Conservation Union and Wetlands International, a new body formed from the International Waterfowl & Wetland Research Bureau, the Asian Wetland Bureau, and America's Wetland Foundation. The Ramsar Convention is thus vitally important in the conservation of the world's wetlands (Barbier et al, 2007).

The Government of India became a contracting/member party of the Ramsar Convention on 1 February 1982 with six wetlands covering 192,973 ha area as internationally important. The Ministry of Environment and Forests (MoEF&CC), Government of India, is the administrative authority for the implementation of the Convention in India. The Ramsar contracting parties are committed to implementing the objectives of the Convention mainly to designate suitable wetlands for the list of international importance (Ramsar List) and ensure their effective management. The 160 contracting parties designated 1953 wetland sites for the Ramsar List, which covers a total surface area of 190,455,433 ha. India has 25 wetlands in the Ramsar List (Figure 2.5) (Sarkar, 2011)

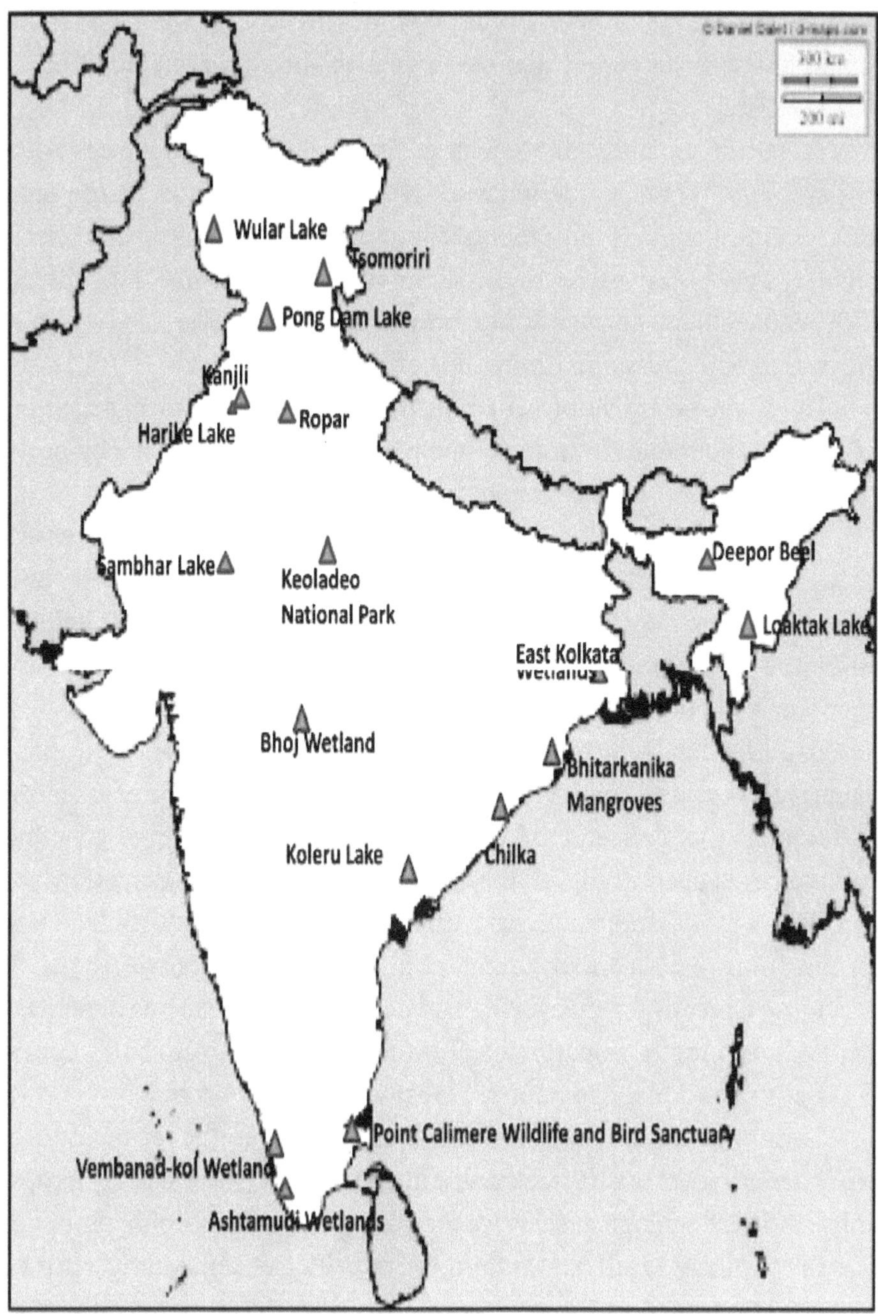

▲ **Figure 2.5:**   Wetlands in India in the Ramsar List

Source: Sarkar, 2011

The present study has been undertaken in and around the Pallikaranai Marsh and it is suggested that this area also should be included in the Ramsar List.

Valuation is only one element in the effort to improve the management of environmental resources such as wetlands. At the same time, decision-makers must take account of many competing interests in deciding how best to use wetlands. Economic valuation may help inform such management decisions, but only if decision-makers are aware of the overall objectives and limitations of valuation.

The main objective of valuation in assisting wetland management decisions is generally to indicate the overall economic efficiency of the various competing uses of wetland resources.

The economic valuation of wetlands is an attempt to assign quantitative values to the goods and services provided by them even if market prices are not available to assist (Barbier et. al., 1997). It helps to assess the relative efficiency of various alternative uses of wetlands and to choose the option that yields maximum net benefits to society.

To understand why economic valuation may be important to wetland management and policy, it is necessary first to review the role of valuation in decisions that concern the use of environmental resources generally and wetlands specifically. A major reason for excessive depletion and conversion of wetland resources is often the failure to account adequately for their non-market environmental values in development decisions. By providing a means for measuring and comparing the various benefits of wetlands, economic valuation can be a powerful tool to aid and improve the wise use and management of global wetland resources.

Constanza et al (1989) opine that the economic evaluation of ecosystems becomes a difficult and subjective exercise especially because of the indirect ecological services that they provide. No doubt, any such exercise is likely to attract quite a bit of criticism depending both on the viewers' as well as the analysts' perceptions. However, the fact that this kind of exercise is gradually becoming more and more imperative cannot be overstated. To give a simple example, in India, there are places where wetlands are being converted to different land use classes, viz. for residential or commercial purposes, and in such cases, the management has to make sure that the envisaged alternative is going to be not only economically beneficial but also ecologically feasible and sustainable. It is under these circumstances that the ecological-economic analysis of wetlands assumes significance.

In India, particularly in Tamil Nadu, the urban wetlands, or the wetlands that are lying near the urban areas, face intense pressure in the form of the threat of degradation due to the increasing urban population and the consequent increase in demand for land. Another problem is the threat of pollution. It has been noted that the main reason for excessive depletion and conversion of wetland resources is the failure to properly account for their values, particularly, the non-use and functional values (Barbier et. al., 1997). Since wetlands are common property resources, it is an uphill task to protect or conserve the wetlands unless the stakeholders who are around the wetland are involved in the process.

In India, the economic valuation of wetlands has been carried out in the recent past in the Bhoj Wetland, Bhopal, East Calcutta Wetland in West Bengal, and Kol Wetland in Kerala. The studies on the valuation of wetlands for non-market goods with the help of the stakeholders in and around the wetlands have not been carried out in Tamil Nadu, especially for Pallikaranai Marsh (urban wetland) which is being taken up in the present study. The lack of awareness about the ecological value of the wetland leads to the indiscriminate use of the wetland. The present study has undertaken a contingent valuation method to assess the Willingness to Pay (WTP) of the urban stakeholders in and around the wetland for the conservation and management of the wetland.

DESCRIPTION OF THE STUDY LOCATION: PALLIKARANAI MARSH

INTRODUCTION

Wetlands are among the most valuable ecosystems in the world and are useful for improving water quality, storing floodwaters, and releasing it slowly as it travels downstream. Wetlands are transition zones between uplands and deeper water; they are unique ecosystems that serve as a home for diverse and fragile living organisms. Wetland systems, directly and indirectly, support lakhs of people, providing goods and services to them, and have numerous other functions. Moreover, wetlands provide habitat for wildlife and open space to promote recreation (Melesse et al, 2007).

Since the signing of the international convention on wetlands at Ramsar in the year 1971, wetlands across the globe have been conserved. The city of Chennai, as it is well known, is a conglomerate of traditional fishing hamlets and villages that were interspersed with settlements that thrived on agriculture and pastoralism. The natural buffer to the human habitations was provided by tracts of littoral forests and wetland complexes. This historical fact is provided by Baden Powell's account of revenue settlements in the Madras Presidency (Menon, 2004). Staying true to the typology, a large part of South Chennai is a flood plain as evidenced by the soil type of the region, which is described as recent alluvium with some exposures of gneiss. It comprises of a large marsh, i.e., Pallikaranai Marsh, smaller satellite wetlands, large tracts of pasture land, and patches of dry forests (Vencatesan, 2007). The region is primarily a marsh type of wetland and demonstrates an overall flat topography with a gentle gradient to the south. The Velachery part of the wetland is the origin of the run-off in the north, and several channels regulate the flow of water in the region. The slope is toward the south and it drains the water from the northern side in Velachery and the hills on the west and southwest of Nanmangalam, Pallavaram, and St. Thomas Mount toward the southern extremes, finally finding way toward the Kovalam Creek. If the sandbar that forms at the mouth of the Kovalam Estuary is not breached regularly, the region faces imminent flooding (NEERI, 1999). While the importance of the South Chennai floodplain is not being undermined, the current study is focused on the Pallikaranai Marsh, which has the distinction of being part of the wetlands that have been identified by the Government of India as priority sites in the National Wetland Conservation Programme, 2010. The marsh helps recharge the aquifers of the region (Jaykumar et al, 2009).

Locally known as *Kazhiveli* (a generic Tamil name for marshes and swamps), the Pallikaranai Marsh drains about 250 sq. km, through two outlets, viz. the Okkiyam Madavu (channel) in Okkiyam Thuraipakkam and the Kovalam Creek. It is imperative that the term *draining* is to be understood in the context of flood mitigation, groundwater recharge, and irrigation.

The Pallikaranai Wetland came into existence as a salt marsh created by the backwaters of the Bay of Bengal. With the construction of the Buckingham Canal in 1876, the inflow of seawater virtually stopped; thereafter the copious inflow of rainwater turned the marsh into a freshwater body. The marsh helps recharge the aquifers of the region. Even today, though some of the water bodies are encroached or abandoned, the rain/drain water flows into this Pallikaranai Marshland. It is a natural formation of a low-lying inland freshwater marsh adjacent to the Bay of Bengal and situated about 20 km south of Chennai city.

The Pallikaranai Marsh is among the few and last remaining natural wetlands of the Coromandel Coast in South India. It is a part of the Perungudi and Pallikaranai villages of Kancheepuram District. The general terrain of the area is plain with an average altitude of about 5 m above mean sea level (Figure 3.1 and Figure 3.2).

The Pallikaranai Marsh is approximately 15 km south of the heart of the city and approximately 4 km of the Chennai city boundary within the Chennai Metropolitan Area's southern boundary. The wetland runs along the Old Mahabalipuram Road, parallel to the Buckingham Canal throughout its length. The marsh is situated adjacent to Velachery, also known as Vedashreni, a rapidly developing residential area in the southwest of Chennai. While Velachery is located toward the northwest of this marsh, Taramani is toward the north, Perungudi to the northeast, Madipakkam to the west, Perumbakkam to the southwest, and Sholinganallur toward the southeast. Surplus water from the 31 tanks situated in three directions, namely north, west, and south of the marsh, drains into the marsh, flows through Okkium Maduvu into the Buckingham Canal, and drains into the Bay of Bengal near Muttukkadu Creek (Figure 3.3) (Figure3.4).

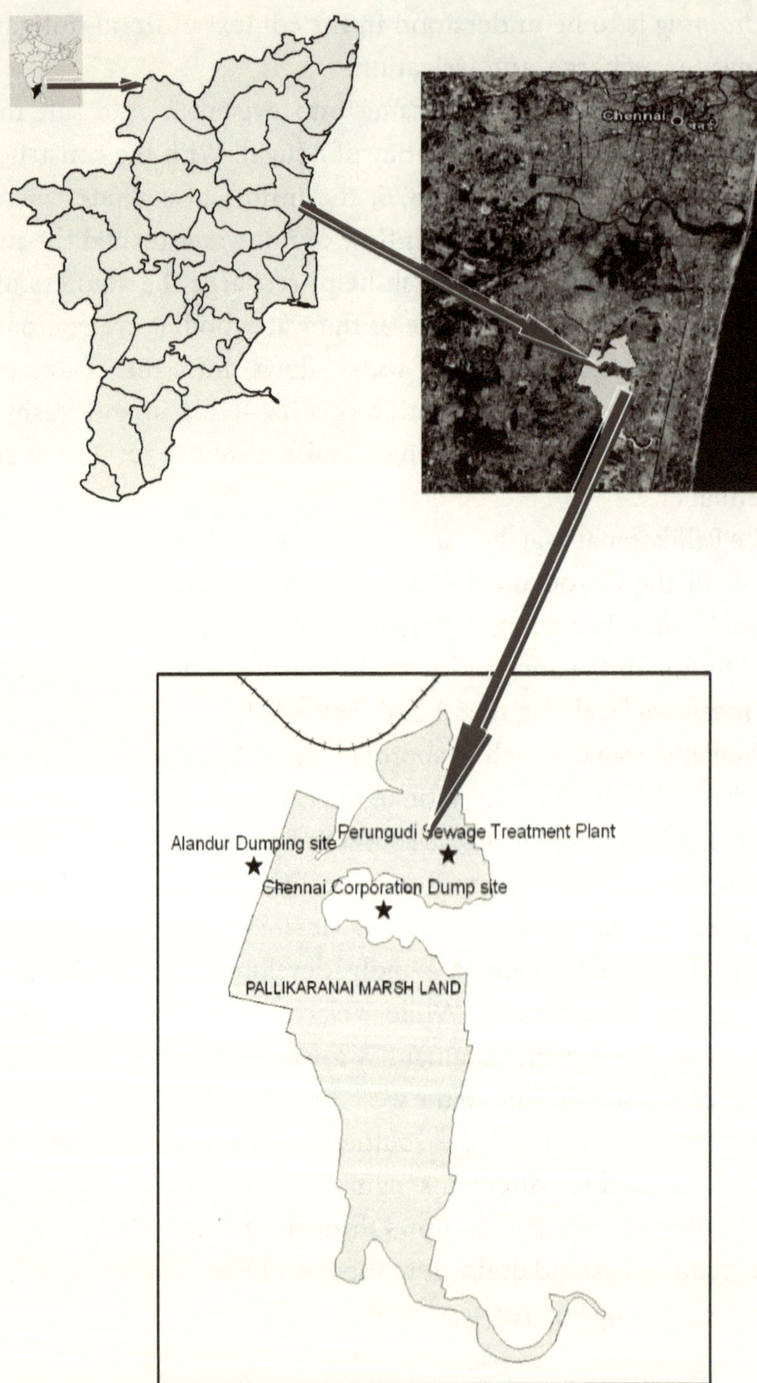

▲ **Figure 3.1:** Location of Pallikaranai Marshland

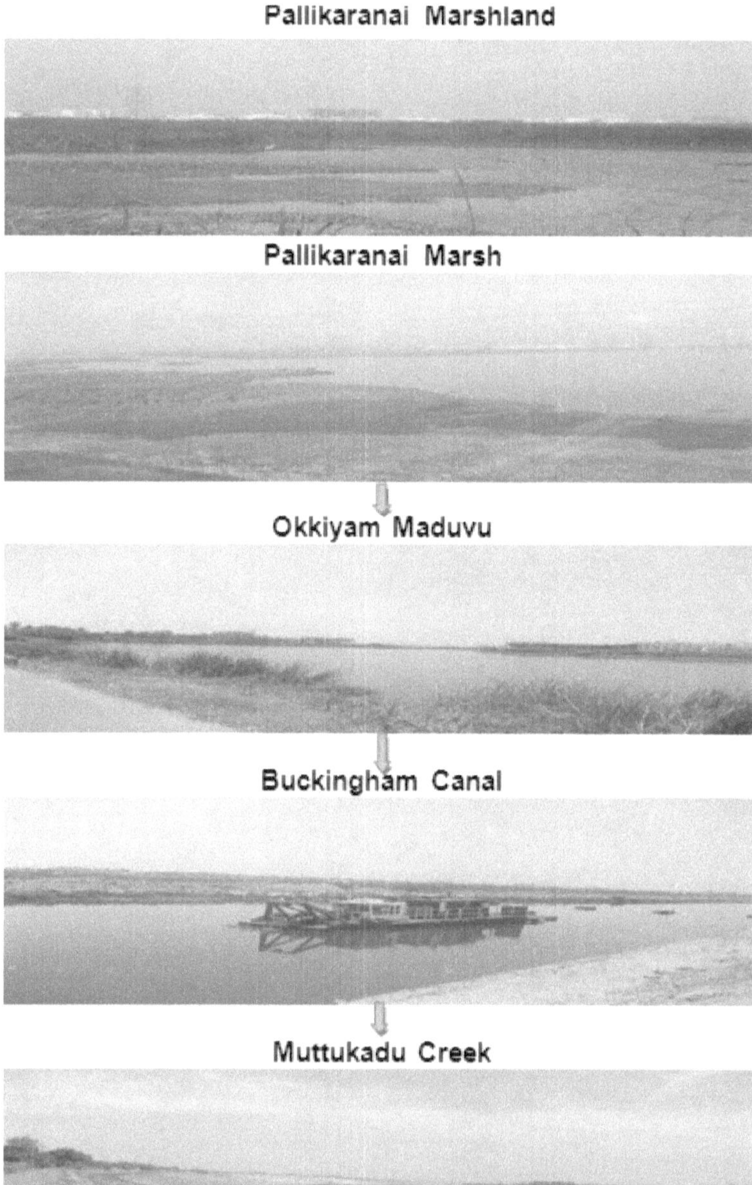

Source: Tamil Nadu Forests Department

▲ **Figure 3.2:** Journey of Water from Pallikaranai Marsh to Bay of Bengal

Source: photographs taken between 2008-2010

▲ **Figure 3.3:** Catchment Area of Pallikaranai Marsh Surrounded By Habitats, It Parks, Multinational Companies, Institutions, and Hospitals

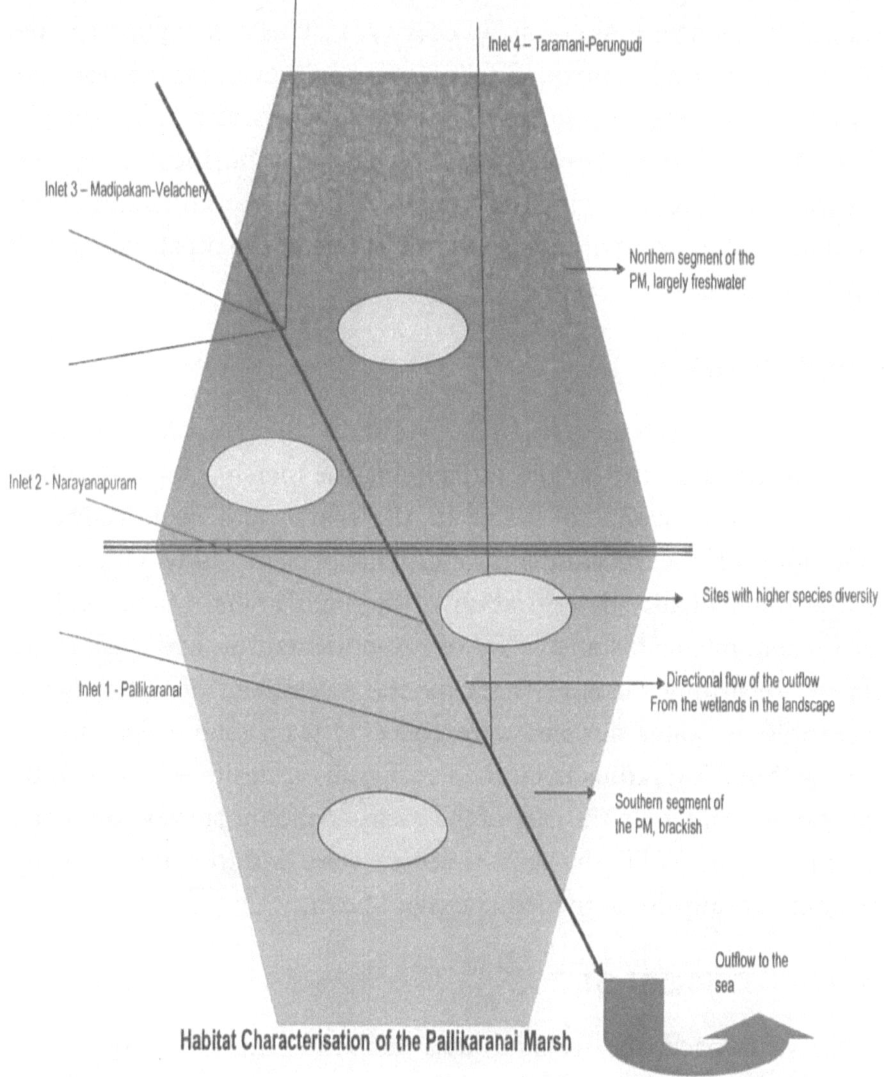

▲ **Figure 3.4:** Habitat Characterization of Pallikaranai Marsh

Source: Care Earth Trust, Chennai.

Pallikaranai Marshland is considered internationally important as it contains a representative of rare or endangered, threatened species. This freshwater marshland is situated very near to one of the cosmopolitan cities of India (Chennai), amidst dense population.

It acts as a forage and breeding ground for thousands of migratory waterbirds from various countries every year. This marsh plays a major role in the natural control, amelioration, or prevention of flooding, seasonal water retention for wetlands, mitigating water pollution, and acting as a natural wastewater and drainage water purification system. It is responsible for charging the aquifers of the region and maintaining a suitable habitat for wildlife by acting as one of the most biologically diverse systems.

STUDY LOCATION

The study is focused on areas in and around Pallikaranai Marsh, taking into consideration the factors influencing the marsh, such as the land use/land cover, quality of water in the marsh and socio-economic conditions of the respondents, etc. The present study emphasizes on the water quality deterioration in the Pallikaranai Marsh and the socio-economic status and WTP of respondents who live close to the Marsh. Regarding the study area for the assessment of water quality deterioration, water samples were collected from tube wells and dug wells within 2 km radius from the Perungudi dumpsite, which is in the Pallikaranai Marsh. In the case of the socio-economic survey conducted to estimate the WTP, the areas selected were within 1 km from the Perungudi dumpsite in the Pallikaranai Marsh.

EXTENT – CURRENT STATUS

A few years back, the wetland area was vast, with plenty of natural macrophytes, lesser weed infestation, and a large number of birds; apparently, it was once a natural haven for a multifold of resident and migratory birds that are seen here currently. At present, due to legalized and illicit encroachments, fast-developing real estate ventures, and various other developments, the haven for these birds is vanishing fast. As more and more information technology parks emerge along the Old Mahabalipuram Road, a large workforce requires accommodation and other basic amenities. Hence, the area around Velachery is booming with real estate projects and pressures are exerted toward the Pallikaranai Marsh. This part of the city, once considered by the public as backward and not favored a few years back, has changed rapidly after the construction of the K T Link Road (under highway department) and the opening of a string of stylish residential projects. The proximity to the airport and development of several roads that cut down the commuting time to the heart of the city has made this area a reaping ground for the real estate business (Azeez et al, 2007) (Figure3.3).

PHYSIOGRAPHY

Land Tenure/Ownership: Glaser et al, (2008) investigated risk assessment of extreme precipitation in the coastal areas of Chennai city. Remote sensing data from different slices were used to analyze the changes in settlement areas. These were combined with long-term meteorological precipitation data for showing the relation between rainfall and the extent of the water bodies in dry, normal, wet, and years of extreme rainfall. The results revealed that the combination of the precipitation data with the extent of the main water body emphasizes that the flood risk in the south of Chennai is increasingly due to man-made changes in the area of Pallikaranai Marsh. In a study that estimated the area and extent of the Pallikaranai Marsh, Care Earth, 2000 reported that the Marsh was historically spread over an area of approximately 5500–6000 ha. Vencatesan (2007) reported that by 2002, the Marsh had lost about 90% of its original extent and was spread over only 593 ha. At present, 317 ha of wetland area is with the State Forest Department, 54.21 ha with the State Public Works Department, and 170.40 ha with the Chennai Corporation; thus a total area of a single water body of 541.61 ha is proposed for a Ramsar site by the Forests Department in the year 2011. The surrounding area has the habitants, corporation patta, educational institutions, IT parks, etc. (Figure 3.5).

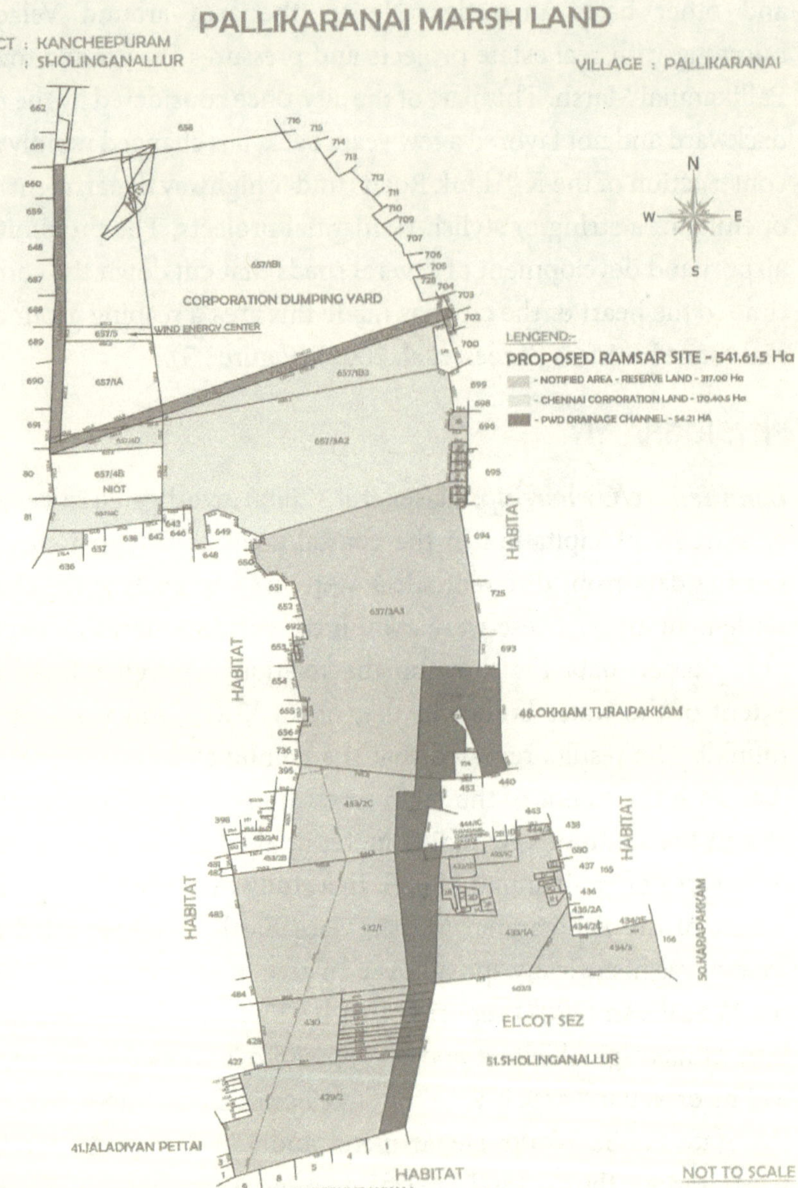

▲ **Figure 3.5:** Pallikaranai Marshland

Source: Tamil Nadu Forest Department

GEOLOGY AND SOIL TYPE

The region is primarily a marsh type of wetland and demonstrates an overall flat topography with a gentle gradient to the south. The wetland at Pallikaranai is an extensive low-lying area, covered by a mosaic of aquatic grass species, scrub, marsh, and water-filled depressions. The general terrain of the area is plain with an average altitude of about 5 m above mean sea level. The substrate in the entire region is made up of the weathered Charnockite bedrock covered with a layer of alluvial soil of varying thickness (Patnaik and Srihari, 2004).

pH Value: Water quality analysis of the Marsh indicates that the pH values range between 6.5 to 8.4. The mild alkaline nature suggests that approximately 95% of CO_2 in water is present as bicarbonate (Jameel and Sirajudeen, 2006). The analysis of pH variation between different time periods does not reveal any notable difference in the study area.

RAINFALL

The climate is clearly divided into pre- and post-monsoon. The southwest monsoon prevails from July to September and the northeast monsoon is active during November, December, and January. Temperature varies seasonally with summer values ranging from 35 to 42 degrees Celsius and winter maximum ranging from 25 to 34 degrees Celsius (Patnaik and Srihari, 2004).

Recharge: Rainfall recharge is the main source of aquifer replenishment. The water level rises during the northeast monsoon period in the months of November to January. The recharge potential of the region is immense as the region is proximate to the South Chennai aquifer. The drainage pattern of marsh and fringe area is highly governed by the tidal level variation in the Buckingham Canal and nature of storm surges. The marsh helps recharge the aquifers of the region. It is one of the last few remaining natural ecosystems in the city of Chennai.

Water: The wetland gets plenty of water input during the monsoons each year. Drainage channels from Velachery, Madipakkam, and Kilkattalai are the main water inlets. Water from the Velachery Lake enters through channels located beneath the bridge near MRTS on the Velachery–Tambaram road. Water from Ullagaram, Puzhudivakkam, Krishna Nagar, and Balaji Nagar enters through the culvert across the Velachery–Tambaram road, immediate to the south of the Velachery Bridge. The stormwater flows from areas of Tirusulam, Old Pallavaram, and Madipakkam and enters the marsh through another canal located further south before the Kilkattalai–Thoraipakkam Road. Waters from Kilkattalai, Narayanapuram, and vicinity flows into the marsh through a channel adjacent to the National Institute of Ocean Technology (NIOT) (Azeez et al, 2007).

However, all channels that collect water discharge into the unprotected area, which currently is practically isolated from the protected area by the K T Link road that bisects the Pallikaranai Marsh. Okkium Maduvu, the channel that empties into the sea through the Buckingham Canal, lies in the protected part. This situation results in high flood water levels during the monsoons in the unprotected region of the marsh and adjacent areas. It also results in the accumulation of nutrients and toxic waste there. The deficient water that flows to the protected part may speed up the ecological succession and may lead to the drying up of the marsh.

Water Quality: The water in the Marsh showed high Total Dissolved Solids (TDS). One of the prominent features of the water quality of Pallikaranai wetlands is the high coliform count. The high TDS level is probably because of effluents and the presence of coliform is due to contamination from human excreta. A low-level presence of heavy metals such as cadmium, chromium, and mercury in the wetland water was also reported (Care Earth 2002).

Hydrological Values: Hydrological values describe the functions and values of the wetland in groundwater recharge, flood control, sediment trapping, shoreline stabilization, etc. The reed-covered swamps and several associated smaller waterlogged areas located in

South Chennai help in storing stormwater and aid in groundwater recharge. It is reported that more than 500 truckloads of drinking water, obviously an outcome of the recharge of groundwater effectuated by the wetland, is collected daily by private operators from the vicinity. This practice is reportedly being still continued. Critical to the existence of this wetland is the exchange of fresh and saline water facilitated through various channels of South Chennai and Okkium Maduvu in Thoraipakkam. Several small wetlands, many of which are under the threat of filling, are sustained by fluvial interactions with the Pallikaranai Marsh.

BIODIVERSITY

The topography of the marsh is such that it always retains some storage, thus forming an aquatic ecosystem. A study by SACON in 2007 has revealed that Pallikaranai Marsh has been a home for naturally occurring plants (more than 60 species), fish (more than 45 species), birds (more than 100species), butterflies (7 species), reptiles (about 20 species), amphibians (about nine species) and several species of molluscs and crustaceans (Annexure II) (Azeez et al, 2007).

Flora

A unique range of adaptations to survive and exploit the wetland environment are visible by the wetland plants (hydrophytes) as they can very well adapt to changing water conditions, high salt, and low oxygen environments. These adaptable plants are categorized into three sections. a. Emergent Plants b. Hygrophytes c. Surface Floaters and Submerged Plants (Patnaik and Srihari, 2004) (Annexure I). Of the 15 grass species recorded from the marsh, at least two, namely *Cynodon barberi* and *Iseilema anthephoroides*, are endemic to Peninsular India. A wild variety of rice (*Oryza* sp.) is also reported from this area (Care Earth, 2005). Some exotic floating vegetation such as water hyacinth and water lettuce are also found, which are now extensive and form thick mats and are highly spread (Figure 3.6).

Turnera ulmifolia L.

Alternanthera paronychioides A.St.Hill

Ipomoea aquatic Forsskal

Pergularia daemia (Forsskal) Chiov.

Ricinus communis L.

Solanum xanthocarpum Sch.

▲ **Figure 3.6:** Floral Species in Pallikaranai Marshland

The species inventory was carried using an ad-hoc method of floristic surveying (Jayakumar et al, 2009). An ad-hoc floristic survey was conducted in the present study starting from the perimeter of the marshland boundaries and circling inside and recording all species. Flora of the Presidency of Madras by Gamble, (1967) was followed for species identification. It was found that a total of 90 species belonging to 77 genera of 36 families are present in the marsh. Out of the 36 families identified, the *Euphorbiaceae* family having six genera belongs to nine species, and *Poaceae* family having seven genera belonging to eight species. (CCC & AR Report, 2011). These species are biogeographically important to the several faunal species that depend on this marshland for roosting, for bird nesting, for host plants for butterflies/flies, for water purifying purposes, to preserve earth cover and they possess high medicinal value.

Fauna

Compared to flora, the biodiversity of fauna is very low. This is due to its extinction from high pollution levels. Low faunal presence indicates advanced stages of wetland degradation. Some species are exterminated, some others mutate while others just migrate.

The wetland is rich in faunal species (Figure 3.7). It is home to ten species of mammals, 112 species of birds, 21 species of reptiles, nine species of amphibians, 46 species of fish, seven species of butterflies, five species of crustaceans, and nine species of molluscs (Annexure II). The swamp also serves as a heronry and wintering ground for migratory birds. In a short field survey conducted by SACON during the first week of March, about 700 little grebes, 150 black-winged stilts, and 150 Asian-pied starlings were recorded. The recent finding of white-spotted garden skink from the land area of this marsh is a new record for Tamil Nadu. Besides, the windowpane oyster, mud crab, mullet, halfbeak, and green chromide are some of the estuarine organisms present at the marsh (Care Earth, 2002).

▲ **Figure 3.7:** Faunal Species in Pallikaranai Marsh

FAUNAL SPECIES IN PALLIKARANAI MARSH   (Continued)

Peasant Tailed Jacana

Moorhen

Yellow Wattled Lapwing

Purple Heron

Yellow Wagtail

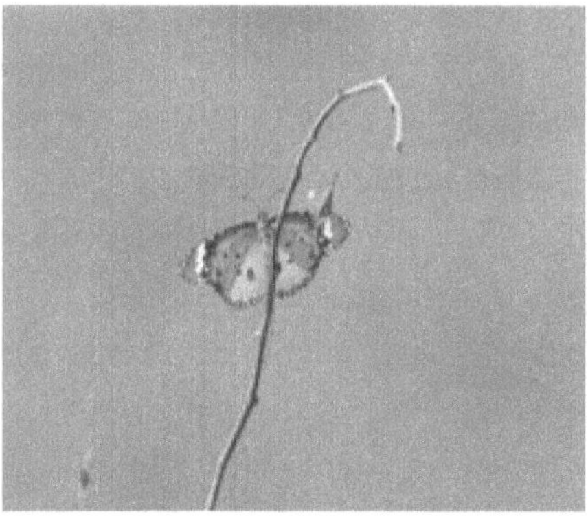

Butterfly

▲ **Figure 3.7:**   (Continued)

Wetlands all over the world act as a wintering spot for many migratory fowls. Much of our knowledge of wetlands as habitat has been derived from the study of birds (Vijayan et al, 2004). In all, 63 species of birds were found in and around the wetland area. The number of birds is expected to rise following the monsoons. The most dominant species is the Indian moorhen (*Gallinula chloropsus*). This bird is found only in a small number in Vedanthangal, a bird sanctuary situated about 50 km from Chennai. These wetlands serve as an ideal habitat for this species because of the *Typha*, a type of tall grass that provides it with the food required and material to build its nest.

The recent finding of the white-spotted garden skink from the land area of this marsh is a new record for Tamil Nadu. Fishes such as dwarf gourami and chromides, which are widely bred and traded worldwide for aquaria, naturally occur in Pallikaranai Wetland.

PRESENT STATE OF THE WETLANDS

There are two major solid urban waste disposal dumps in the region. The first is the large Perungudi Sewage Treatment Plant (STP) of the Chennai Metro Water and Sewage Supply Board (CMWSSB), which has the capacity of handling 45 million liters a day (MLD) of garbage. The other is the Alandur Municipality dump yard on the Velachery-Medavakkam Road. It handles a garbage load of 80-100 tons a day. The garbage at the moment is being dumped into the dump yard, which is largely a wetland and whose depth used to be almost 15 feet; now it has been filled to a depth of 7 feet. Apart from this, the Alandur Municipality Sewage Treatment Plant is also coming up within Perungudi with an installed capacity of 25 MLD. These dump yards are a major menace for the region as they profusely pollute the area by producing foul odor and attract stray dogs and birds. Burning of the waste causes respiratory problems to the local community and affects the biota of the region (Azeez et al, 2007).

As reported by Care Earth (2005), the wetland is rich with several plant species including 61 species of flowering plants. (Annexure II). The

Pallikaranai Marshland also provides shelter to two near-threatened bird species, namely spot-billed pelican (*Pelecanus philippensis*) and black-headed ibis (*Threskiornis melanocephalus)* (Raj et al, 2010) (Figure3.7).

ECOLOGICAL IMPORTANCE

In recent years, several studies with more or less related objectives were conducted in Pallikaranai Marsh. Various studies conducted in the marsh summarize that the reed-covered swamps and several associated smaller waterlogged areas located in South Chennai help in storing and aiding groundwater recharge. Critical to the existence of this wetland is the exchange of fresh and saline water facilitated through various channels of South Chennai and Okkium Maduvu in Thoraipakkam. Several small wetlands, many of which are under the threat of filling, are sustained by fluvial interactions with the Pallikaranai Marsh. The profusely growing Typha and other aquatic macrophytes serve as bio-filter for pollutants discharged into the wetland (Azeez et al, 2007).

Pallikaranai Marsh is a source of income for many locals. The inhabitants of Pallikaranai, Taramani, Velachery, Perungudi, Perumbakkam, Thoraipakkam, and Sholingannalur partially depend on the wetland for subsistence. Of these, some ethnic groups are highly reliant on the wetland. During the summer season, the local people use this marsh for fishing. The fishermen are dependent on the wetland, whereas the Adi-Dravidars are partially dependent on the wetland. Their direct economic activities include gathering reed, fishing, etc.

The surrounding habitats of Pallikaranai Marsh let off the drainage water into the marshland. The treated effluent from Perungudi Effluent Treatment Plant is let off into the marsh. Thus, the marsh mitigates water pollution and acts as a natural wastewater and drainage water purification system. It plays a major role in the natural control, amelioration, or prevention of flooding. It acts as a natural recharge of aquifers and major natural flood plain system of the region. It acts as a forage and breeding ground for thousands of migratory waterbirds from various countries every year (Azeez et al, 2007).

Pallikaranai Marshland is considered important as it contains a representative of rare or endangered, threatened species. This freshwater marshland is situated very near to one of the cosmopolitan cities of India (Chennai) amidst of dense population. The Pallikaranai Marsh is ecologically very important and several small wetlands, many of which are under the threat of filling, are sustained by fluvial interactions with the Pallikaranai Marsh. The marsh acts as natural wastewater and drainage water purification system, natural recharge of aquifers, and is the major natural flood plain system of the region.

ENVIRONMENTAL DEGRADATION, THREATS, RELATED KEY ISSUES AND CHANGES IN LAND USE WITH RESPECT TO PALLIKARANAI MARSH

INTRODUCTION

Wetlands are one of the most threatened habitats in the world. According to the UN Millennium Ecosystem Assessment (2005), environmental degradation is more prominent within wetland systems when compared to other natural systems of the earth. This degradation is spread over a range of habitat types that are known under the generic category of wetlands; viz. mangroves, paddy fields, or lakes. The degradation is due to factors such as the process of ill-planned urbanization, industrialization, and encroachments. Wetland ecosystems provide innumerable tangible and intangible benefits to society, but somehow they remain away from the domain of the market force (Dugan, 1990).

Indeed, despite various forms of international and national legislation ratifying their protection, wetlands continue to be affected by human activities, including channelization, drainage, crop production, effluent disposal, and water obstruction. Barbier et al (1997); Turner et al (2000).

According to the Ramsar Database, 84% of Ramsar listed wetlands had been affected by ecological change by 1999. Worldwide, around 50% of wetlands are estimated to have disappeared since 1900. During the first half of the previous century, this mostly occurred in the northern temperate zones. However, since the 1950s, tropical and sub-tropical wetlands are the latest victims. The main reasons for continuing wetland degradation are economic development and inconsistencies in government policies. Mechanisms such as embanking a river, overexploitation of groundwater resources, or building dams are only a few of many reasons why wetlands are deteriorating. Pollution from agricultural and industrial sources increases levels of nutrients, pesticides, and heavy metals which seriously impair ecological processes. Most wetland habitats are extremely vulnerable and highly biodiverse with many threatened fish, amphibians, and other species.

Wetlands in India, as elsewhere, are increasingly facing several anthropogenic pressures. Significant losses have resulted from their conversion threats from industrial, agricultural, and various urban developments. These have led to hydrological perturbations, pollution, and their effects. Unsustainable levels of grazing and fishing activities have also resulted in the degradation of wetlands (Prasad et al, 2002).

The State of Tamil Nadu has a number of water bodies and wetlands. Several of these are facing serious threats or are increasingly disappearing due to multifarious pressures. This is especially true for those wetlands located close to growing urban centers or bustling metropolises. The population growth is so intense due to migrants, pressure on the local infrastructure, ecological fragmentation, poverty, air pollution, catastrophic waste and sewage management, improper drainage systems, and inadequate water supply leading to disastrous seasonal floods, diseases, groundwater lowering, pollution and environmental destruction (Drescher et al. 2007).

Pallikaranai Marsh is one of the last few remaining natural ecosystems in the city of Chennai. This wetland is located on the outskirts of Chennai. It is one such wetland that is very likely to disappear in the near future if active appropriate interventions are not made now (Glaser et al, 2006). Out of 566.59 ha of Pallikaranai Marsh, an area of 317.00 ha of marsh has been declared as Pallikaranai Marsh Reserved Land under Tamil Nadu Forest Act 1882 with effect from 18.04.2007.

ENVIRONMENTAL CHANGE OF THE PALLIKARANAI MARSH

Marshlands can be divided into freshwater marshes and saltwater marshes. Saltwater marshes are relatively stable ecosystems due to the influence of saltwater and specific specialized aquatic fauna. Purely freshwater marshes on the other hand are transitional and in the process of changing into terrestrial grassland. Once they have transitioned into a terrestrial land, the change is nearly irreversible. The extreme progression of urbanization dynamics around a marsh has a dramatic influence on the ecosystem of the marshland. Fragmentation, a decrease of water spread, the introduction of invasive plants, and intense pollution gravely alter water ecology and dynamics. The consequence is the initiation of a change from a mainly saltwater marshland to a terrestrial land.

From the previous literature on Pallikaranai Marsh, it is seen that the fragmentation of the marsh was the division of the overflow area on the east side of Okkiyam Maduvu through the construction of Buckingham Canal about 100-150 years ago by the East India Company. Historically, there was a natural connection between the Marshland and the Bay of Bengal by which saltwater could spread into the marsh and reciprocally run-off into the sea. After the construction, the overflow area was divided and only a small connection was allowed between the marsh and the saltwater sea.

This decreased saltwater influence and also decreased freshwater drainage into the sea; a secondary marsh was formed with the creation of the floodplain southeast to Pallikaranai and west of Buckingham Canal. The primary marshland, hence, was divided into southern and northern parts. The south part was primarily a saltwater marsh with a tidal saltwater influence that was flooded only seasonally with fresh water. The northern part was within freshwater influence. Two water inlets brought in rainwater which was partly stagnant and drained slowly into the southern part and then into the sea. Due to the seasonal rain variation, it was a seasonal habitat. Velachery consisted, at that point in time, of grassland, scrubland, and artificial woodlot (Guindy National Park). In dry periods, it could be used to graze cattle, while in the wet season, it was a flooded marshland.

Through accelerating urban development, the area of the original marshland decreased and the change in water spread, depth, and pollution brought a change in the aquatic flora. Due to the increasing water depth, plants like *Typha* and *Water hyacinth* emerged, which could spread and displace native submerged flora. Increasing water pollution, sedimentation, and eutrophication gave additional impulses.

The land reclamation has different effects on the surrounding marshland. Clay soil, garbage, and debris used for land reclamation introduce and spread more invasive plants like *Prosopis juliflora*, which in turn promotes the growth of domestic and invasive terrestrial plants leading to terrestrial formations.

THREATS AND RELATED KEY ISSUES WITH RESPECT TO PALLIKARANAI MARSH

Human Population Growth

Chennai and its suburbs experience rapid industrial development, commercial activities, higher employment opportunities, and consequent activities, as Chennai is one of the largest commercial and industrial centers of India. As per the CMWSSB Report in 2007, the population of Chennai city was 4.344 million in the year 2001, while the estimated population for June 2007 was 5.375 million. As per Census 2011, Chennai has a population of 13.68 million within the area administered by the Chennai Corporation and an Extended Metropolitan Area.

Many places that were earlier suburban outskirts, after having got integrated into the city, are centers of high population growth, facing consequential changes in the environment, built-up areas, and land use. Velachery and Pallikaranai areas are among such locations that undergo such changes, facing severe pressures on land resources. Several IT, ITES, and BPOs are opening their new offices at Pallikaranai, owing to which the rate of growth of real estate business is almost around 30%. The road-over-bridge (ROB) project in Tambaram and grade separators at Pallikaranai are boosting the real estate business in the Pallikaranai Panchayat (Azeez et al, 2007).

Encroachments

As per the report of Care Earth in the year 2005, the wetland is gradually being swallowed up by a rapidly flourishing real estate business. Several organizations and housing developments have already occupied considerable portions of the wetland area. This low-lying land near the city offers a harvest for real estate business with the upcoming IT business, hospitals, and proximity to the airport. Other encroachments by small hutments and residential colonies are also common.

The development activities are filling up the marsh at an alarming rate. Dredging undertaken by the Thangavelu Engineering College, located in the southern part of the protected area, has completely interfered with the movement of tidal waters into the marsh. In addition to this, the construction projects like Mass Rapid Transit System (MRTS), NIOT, and Central Wind Energy Technology (CWET) are also located here. Many shopping complexes, transportation, parks, multistoried buildings, hospitals, and educational institutions have also rapidly mushroomed on the marsh area, depleting it (CCC&AR Report, 2011).

Dumping of Solid Waste

According to Esakku et al (2007), the Municipal Solid Waste (MSW) generation in Chennai, has increased from 600 to 3500 tons per day (TPD) within 20 years. The highest per capita solid waste generation rate in India is in Chennai (0.6 kg/d). Chennai Corporation has no proper landfill and the waste is being dumped in two open dumpsites at Perungudi and Kodungaiyur respectively. The dumpyard at Perungudi is at the Pallikaranai Marsh area, which houses a large number of species of plants and animals. Due to the indiscriminate dumping of the past 15 years in this area, almost 25% of the marshland has been lost (Jayakumar et al, 2009).

The Perungudi dump yard is situated in a low-lying and poorly drained area of marshy land, which is permanently wet and seasonally inundated. According to Jaganathan et al (2010), the extent of the dumping area during 1994 was 23.70 ha and the same yard had been expanded to 66.50 ha in 2004 and it is further expanded to 79.20 ha during 2008. As per Chennai Corporation data collected in September 2011, the total area of this site is about 202.00 ha out of which about 32.37 ha is used for dumping. At present, the government has ordered to restrict the dumping of MSWs to about 80.94 ha. The current rate of dumping is 1500-1800 MT/day (Metric tons/day). The quantity of garbage dumped till now is 70 lakhs MT (approx). As there is no treatment done to the municipal waste, the entire quantity of municipal waste has been dumped at this disposal site for the last 20-25 years and is connected with easily accessible roads. At Perungudi dump yard the quantity of waste disposed of is more in the northern section, whereas in the southern part the quantity is relatively less.

Fifteen pumping stations that collect the sewage that is generated in their surrounding environs pump it to the Perungudi STP where it is received through a myriad of pipelines. The design capacity of the STP is 45 MLD. The treated effluents from Perungudi STP are also let off in the marsh. The surrounding habitats also let off the drainage water into the marsh.

According to the data collected from the Corporation of Chennai from the year 2001 to October 2011, the total garbage and debris disposed of in the Perungudi dumping yard increased initially and decreased slowly from 2009-10 to date as shown in Table 4.1 and Figure 4.1. Similarly, the average garbage and debris disposed of in Perungudi dumping yard increased initially and decreased slowly from 2009-10 till date as shown in Table 4.2 and Figure 4.2.

▼ **Table 4.1:** Total Municipal Solid Waste Disposed at Perungudi Dump Yard Per Year

YEAR	GARBAGE	DEBRIS
	METRIC TONS	
2000-01	16994	931.5
2001-02	19036	902.6
2002-03	18926	562.5
2003-04	18823	2473.1
2004-05	20135	2532.9
2005-06	18696	1620.0
2006-07	17142	1252.7
2007-08	17715	985.6
2008-09	22851	1288.5
2009-10	21867	3021.1
2010-11	20715	2659.9

▼ **Table 4.2:** Average Municipal Solid Waste Disposed at Perungudi Dump Yard Per Day

YEAR	GARBAGE	DEBRIS
	METRIC TONS	
2000-01	1416.2	77.6
2001-02	1586.3	75.2
2002-03	1577.2	46.9
2003-04	1568.6	206.1
2004-05	1677.9	211.1
2005-06	1558.0	135.0
2006-07	1428.5	104.4
2007-08	1476.2	82.1
2008-09	1904.3	107.4
2009-10	1822.3	251.8
2010-11	1726.2	221.7

Source: Unpublished data of Corporation of Chennai (year 2001 to October 2011)

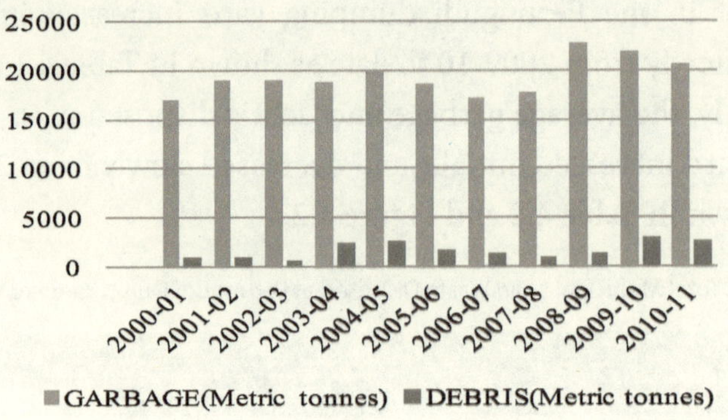

▲ **Figure 4.1:** Total Municipal Solid Waste Disposed at Perungudi Dump Yard Per Year

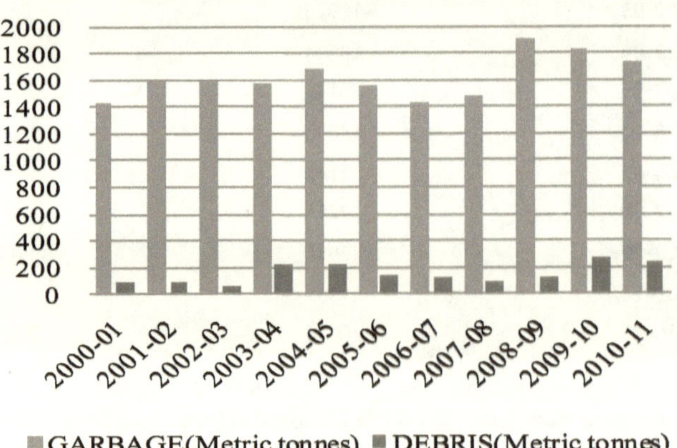

▲ **Figure 4.2:** Average Municipal Solid Waste Disposed at Perungudi Dump Yard Per Day

The Municipal Solid Waste Management (MSWM) is the primary function of the Corporation of Chennai that includes the street sweeping, collection, transportation, and disposal of MSW within the city limits. There are three different organizations, namely the Corporation of Chennai, Onyx, and Civic Exnora that are involved in the MSWM of the city. Chennai is the first city in India to contract out MSWM services to a foreign private agency – Onyx, which is a Singapore-based company. The scope of privatization includes activities such as sweeping, collecting, storing, transporting of MSW, and creating public awareness in three municipal zones. Onyx collects about 1100 metric tons of waste from three zones per day and transports it to open dumps in and around the Pallikaranai Wetland (Azeez et al, 2007). In 2002, Onyx was served with a notice by the TNPCB for dumping wastes indiscriminately in this wetland without designating any area either as a landfill site or with a liner underneath, which may directly pollute the freshwater resources. The TNPCB took exception to the fact that Onyx had failed to demarcate the area allotted for dumping and that the primitive mode of dumping had threatened the wetlands (Sawhney, 2006). Although it is stated that the Municipal Corporation and Onyx are allowed to use 30 ha to dump garbage, Onyx uses about 180 ha for the purpose. About 40 MLD of domestic sewage is also released into the wetland every day (Dams, Rivers and People, 2004).

An Azeez et al (2007) study showed that the garbage dumping site, situated adjacent to the protected part of the Pallikaranai Marsh, has effectively choked over 250 acres of prime marshland. It has fragmented the marsh and obstructed the drainage and flood control potentials of the wetland.

Soil Erosion and Siltation

The Public Works Department (PWD) of Tamil Nadu in its report in the year 2005 showed that the booming real estate business led to massive land modification and uprooting of native vegetation that caused large-scale soil erosion. Rapid urbanization involves land clearing, leveling, and construction activities in the catchment area. The disturbed and loosened surface soil is washed away as a run-off and settled in the low-lying area of the marsh, thus choking macrophytes as well as reducing productivity, water, and sediment quality and subsequently the habitat quality. High siltation is a significant step in the life of a vanishing wetland and is one of the main threats to the existence of the Pallikaranai Marsh.

Roads

The Pallikaranai Marsh is divided into two distinct portions by the K T Link road, which is becoming a dense traffic corridor. The road practically cuts off the continuity of the wetland system. Due to the formation of roads across and around the marsh, the water movement between the two segments of the marsh is stopped. Thus, there are hindrances in the movement of aquatic species, water birds, reptiles, and amphibians across the segments of the marsh. There is also a high accumulation of pathogenic organisms. The roads formed in and around the marsh lead to a higher chance of illicit waste dumping along the roadsides and the unlawful release of effluents. Consequently, there is an increase in the accumulation of pollutants. The formation of roads causes more noise and air pollution due to heavy traffic, which affects especially the avifauna (Azeez et al, 2007).

The key issues relating to the Pallikaranai Marsh are discussed below:

CONSEQUENCES OF HUMAN INTERFERENCE IN PALLIKARANAI MARSH
Increase in Pollutant Levels

The open dumping of waste in the wetland is a significant source of surface water contamination within a short period and subsequently groundwater pollution due to leaching. Once contaminated, it is virtually impossible to clean groundwater. The Perungudi dump yard is a large producer of dioxins and other poisonous gases. Incessant burning of garbage is a sight round the clock near the marsh. Including three carcinogens, 27 chemicals were reported in the air samples analyzed for 69 volatile organic chemicals and 20 sulfur compounds in the area, CEM (2006). Carcinogens such as 1,3-Butadiene, Benzene, and Chloromethane were present at levels of 34782, 2360, and 209 times higher respectively than the levels considered safe by the US Environmental Protection Agency (USEPA).

Most of the garbage is set ablaze after being dumped. Dozens of people, including children, rummage through the smoldering garbage mounds to collect items and material that can be reprocessed or resold. The smoke from burning garbage poses a serious health threat to both the people working in the dumping ground and residents of the area.

Studies in all residential areas skirting the marsh revealed that water at all depths is unfit for human consumption. It was also reported that water in and around the garbage dump had high levels of heavy metals such as mercury, cadmium, and lead (Care Earth, 2002).

Chandramohan and Bharati (2009) opined that the marsh has been contaminated by the discharge of partially treated or untreated sewage water considering it as a wasteland. The CMWSSB has been letting out 32 million liters of untreated sewage water every year directly into the marsh. Even treated sludge discharged into marshland depletes the quality of a marsh.

Loss of Biodiversity

Reduction in the wetland area and in the water and soil quality due to garbage dumping and increased level of pollutants is leading to the visible loss of biodiversity, especially the aquatic flora, and fauna. Avifauna that includes both resident and migratory birds will be visibly affected, particularly by human, vehicular, and machinery disturbances. A study conducted in the year 2002 by Care Earth supported by Tamil Nadu Pollution Control Board (TNPCB) reported only 202 black-winged stilts and 500 cattle egrets of these species respectively in the marsh. It is also reported that many bird species seen common earlier are declining fast in the marsh area. From the study conducted by Patnaik and Srihari (2004), it is evident that these ecological havens of biodiversity are being destroyed due to the negligent development initiatives with rampant human encroachment and unscientific solid waste disposal.

Deterioration of Water Quality

The suburbs of Chennai are expanding rapidly with a huge increase in the influx of population. Long spells of water shortages combined with rapid and haphazard urbanization have led to the overexploitation of the precious water bodies. Mindless dumping of sewage and garbage into the lakes has affected them seriously. Chenna Krishnan et al (2008) found in a study that the quality of water in three important lakes of southern suburban Chennai deteriorated due to encroachments, dumping of wastes, and un-checked inflow of domestic and industrial effluents. In the recent past, concerning the Perungudi dumping yard in Chennai, it was found that the site is subjected to many environmental changes due to leachate occurring around the dumping area. Dipankar and Srihari (2004), opine that the dump yard in the marsh is a major menace for the region as it profusely pollutes the area by producing foul odor and attracts stray dogs, birds. Also, the burning of this causes respiratory problems to the local community and affects the water quality and biota of the region. The leachate coming out from the waste might cause the contamination of the ground and groundwater and in turn change in the physico-chemical properties of soil.

Reduction in Wetland Area

Jaganathan et al (2010), conducted a study on the land use that has changed in the Chennai suburb area due to the conversion of agricultural and wastelands into IT, industries, and settlement expansion. Similarly, Chenna Krishnan et al (2008), studied that, in Chennai, the water spread area derived from Survey of India toposheets during 1975 was 33 sq. km. and has come down to 22.247 sq. km during 2008. The total loss in water spread area in between 1975 and 2008 is 10.753 sq. km. Encroachment in waterways and water spread area is the root cause for loss in water spread area.

Care Earth in 2002, supported by the Tamil Nadu Pollution Control Board (TNPCB), found that the area in Pallikaranai Marsh has been reduced to about 600 ha. Another study by the same agency conducted during 2005 reported further reduction (to 420 ha) of the wetland. About 30% reduction of the wetland area within a span of three years is very alarming. Vencatesan (2007) stated that the marsh had lost 90% of its original extent and was spread over only 593 ha. Hence, due to a rapid decrease in the reduction of area in Pallikaranai Marsh, the area of the marsh for the year 2010 and also for the year 2001 is determined with the help of GIS.

CHANGES IN LAND USE/LAND COVER IN PALLIKARANAI MARSH BETWEEN 1991 AND 2010

About 30 years ago, the Pallikaranai Wetland was spread over an area of more than 5000 ha (50 km^2). The area of the wetland has been decreasing rapidly. Urban development has taken place in very ecologically sensitive zones. The environmental changes that have taken place in Pallikaranai Marsh until the year 2001 are the extreme progression of urbanization dynamics around Pallikaranai Marsh that have a dramatic influence on the ecosystem marshland. Fragmentation, a decrease of water spread, the introduction of invasive plants, and intense pollution gravely alter water ecology and dynamics. The consequence is the initiation of a change from a mainly saltwater marshland to a terrestrial land. Further, gross fragmentation, pollution, and degradation processes are very close to destroying the marshland ecosystem, including important ecosystem services (Figure 4.3).

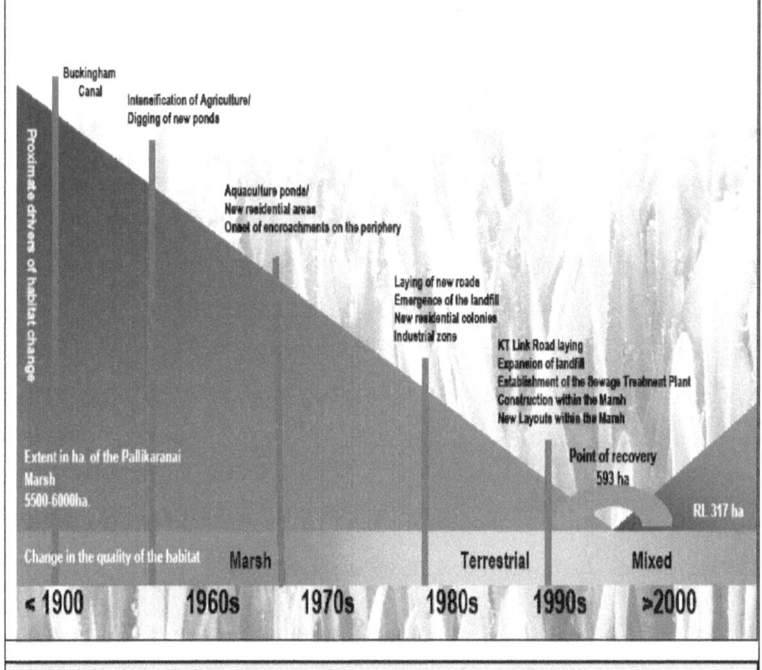

CHANGES IN THE QUALITY OF THE HABITAT IN PALLIKARANAI MARSH

Between 1960 to 1970's, Pallikaranai wetland was a marsh land . Between 1970 to 1980's, it slowly turned to terrestrial habitat. In year 2007, the Tamil Nadu Forests Department had declared 317.00 ha. of Marsh as Pallikaranai Marsh Reserved Land under Tamil Nadu Forest Act 1882 with effect from 18.04.2007.Since then, the point of recovery of the Pallikaranai wetland is seen.

▲ **Figure 4.3:**   Changes in Quality of Habitat in Pallikaranai Marsh

As mentioned in the previous paragraph, the land use/land cover changes are seen for the past 30 years; hence, the present study has used Geographical Information Systems (GIS) and Remote Sensing (RS) tools to study these changes between the year 1990 and 2010. The technical assistance for the present study was from the Centre for Climate Change & Disaster Management (CCC&DM) Anna University, Chennai. Landsat Thematic Mapper (TM) of 1991 and 2010 images covering Pallikaranai wetlands were acquired which in turn were obtained from National Remote Sensing Centre, Hyderabad.

The Landsat Thematic Mapper data is processed using ERDAS IMAGINE 9.3 image processing software. The images are imported into the ERDAS layer stack module to form a floating scene and to group the bands together. Initially, the image of 1991 is geometrically corrected and geo-referenced by using the topography at the scale of 1:50,000. Then the geometrically corrected 1991 image is used as a master image to register other images. This is followed by performing further geometric corrections of the 2010 image to remove a few scattered clouds in the image. The images are projected to the Universal Traverse Mercator (UTM) coordinates Zone 44. The spheroid and datum are also referenced to WGS 84. Accurate geometric registration of an image set with RMSE of <1 is necessary for accurate land use change analysis. After the rectification processes, datasets are cropped based on the detailed polygon area in the study area.

Classification of land use based on multi-spectral or multi-temporal remote sensing images has been the main approach for detecting wetland change. In order to obtain high-quality land use change, ArcGIS software is used for digitization. Supervised classification with a maximum likelihood algorithm was used in this study because this classification algorithm produces consistently good results for most habitat types. The training polygons were digitized on-screen based on terrain knowledge acquired during fieldwork and were distributed throughout the study area. Seven land cover categories were digitized in GIS polygons incorporating (1) Water body and vegetation (2) Settlements (3) Dump yard (4) Sewage treatment plant (5) Grassland. In order to evaluate the accuracy of land use maps derived from remote sensing images covering the Pallikaranai Wetland, a field survey was conducted covering the entire study area using a GPS facility.

After the accuracy assessment, the classified images were exported to the ARC GIS to generate the land cover and land use map. Post classification comparison proved to be an effective technique because data from different dates were separately classified, thereby minimizing the problem of normalizing for atmosphere and sensor differences among dates. Once maps had exactly the same number of feature pixels, they were subjected to a cross tabular comparison. This indicated the differences in the extent of each class and the transitions that had taken place between dates.

The results of the study on the changes in land use/land cover in Pallikaranai Marsh in the year 1991 and the year 2010 are given in Table 4.3 and Table 4.4 and Figure 4.4 and Figure 4.5.

▼ **Table 4.3:** Land Use/land Cover Changes in Years 1991 and 2010

Class	1991 (ha)	2010 (ha)
Wetland (open water, floating vegetation, and emerging vegetation) this is the area with deep water (core area of the Marsh)	592.17	523.33
Settlements	138	1146.28
Dump yard	5.81	66.18
Sewage treatment plant	0	23.52
Grassland	1424.02	401.38

Source: Based on the data compiled by the author

▼ **Table 4.4:** Percentage Of Land Use /land Cover Changes Between Years 1991 and 2010

Class	1991 -2010 (ha)	Change (%)
Wetland (open water, floating vegetation, and emerging vegetation) this is the area with deep water (core area of the Marsh)	-68.84	-11.6
Settlements	1008.28	87.96
Dump yard	60.37	91.22
Sewage treatment plant	23.52	1
Grassland	-1022.64	-71.81

Source: Based on the data compiled by the author

In Table 4.3, it is seen that the area under the wetland and grassland has decreased, whereas the area under the settlements and dump yard area has increased tremendously between 1991 and 2010.

In Table 4.4, it is seen that the increase in the settlements is from 138 ha in 1991 to 1146 ha in 2010, that is,% change by 87.96%. Due to the rapid urbanization, the wastes generated in the major part of Chennai city are being dumped in the marsh; as a result, the marsh has witnessed an increase in dump area by 60.37 ha and% change by 91.22%. The Sewage Treatment Plant (STP) in the marsh area was under operation from 2006 under the CCRCP scheme; hence, in the year 2010, 23.52 ha was under the STP. There was a rapid decrease in grassland from 1424.02 ha in 1991 to 401.38 ha in the year 2010 and% change by -71.81%.

The Pallikaranai Wetland is being eaten up by the rampant urban sprawl and unscientific solid waste disposal. From the previous studies conducted by Patnaik and Srihari (2004), Chandramohan, and Bharathi (2009) and Jaykumar et al (2009), it was seen that there was a tremendous reduction in the area of the marsh.

Jaykumar et al (2009), opined that the satellite-based study on the wetland showed that 45.54% of wetland area had been converted into various forms of land use between 1991 and 2001. Encroachment is a major threat, which is responsible for 83% of land conversion. The garbage dump and road construction are responsible for the remaining 17% of conversion. The rate of conversion of wetland to other land use is at the rate of 97.37 ha per year.

Moreover, between 1991 and 2001, a bypass road was constructed, dividing the marsh into two halves and arresting the water movements, which occupied 46.39 ha. Similarly, in the present study on Pallikaranai Marsh, on comparing the land use/land cover maps in the years 1991 and 2010, (Figures 4.4 and 4.5), the reduction in the area of Pallikaranai Marsh is seen distinctly and the magnitude of reduction is also alarming.

The land use pattern for the years 1991 and 2010 respectively shows that there is a significant increase in settlements, which increased from 138 ha in 1991 to 1146.28 ha in 2010 which is an 87.96% increase. Due to rapid urbanization in the Velachery area and also due to the waste generated in the major part of the Chennai city being dumped inside the marsh (in Perungudi dump yard), the marsh has clearly witnessed an increase in dump area by 91.22% between years 1990 to 2010. A rapid decrease in the area of grassland from 1424.02 to 401.38 ha in 2010 indicated that human activities strengthened the disturbance of the Wetland.

To sum up, Pallikaranai Marsh is one of the important urban wetlands in India, which acts as a giant water aquifer, safeguarding the city against floods in the southern part of Chennai. But this has now been seriously compromised due to the garbage dumping and rampant development along the fringes of the marsh. It was seen that the wetland area and grasslands decreased and the area under settlements and dump yard increased between the years 1990 to 2010. This contributes to water pollution in the marshland leading to the deterioration of water quality, which is the subject matter of the following chapter.

LAND USE/ LAND COVER 1991

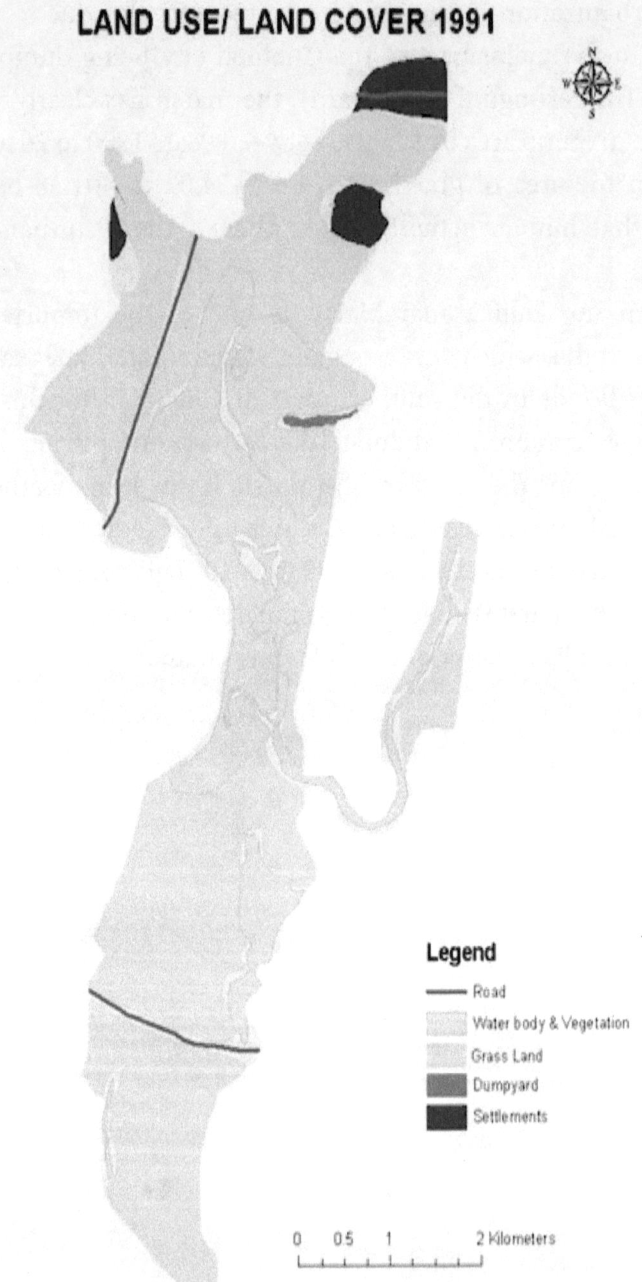

▲ **Figure 4.4:**   Land Use /land Cover Map for Pallikaranai Marsh Area in Year 1991

Source: Based on the data compiled by Author

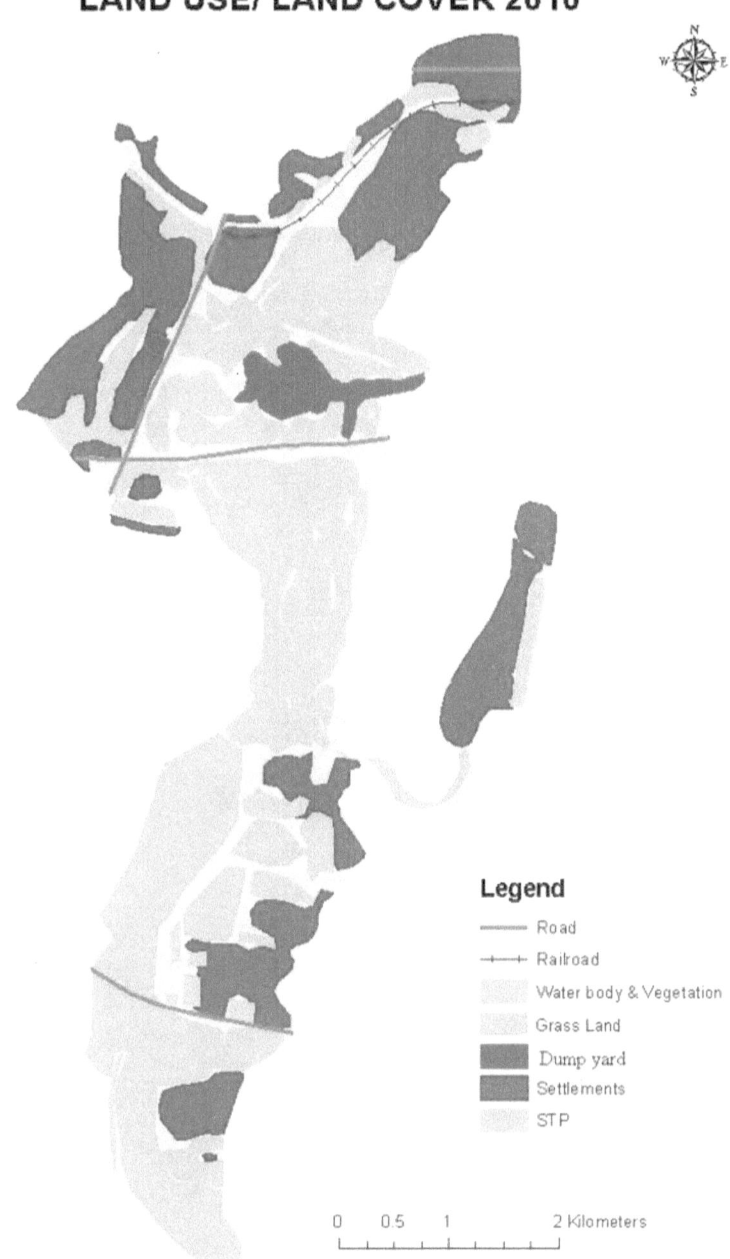

▲ **Figure 4.5:** Land Use /land Cover Map for Pallikaranai Marsh Area in Year 2010

Source: Based on the data compiled by Author

WATER POLLUTION AND DETERIORATION OF WATER QUALITY IN THE PALLIKARANAI MARSH

INTRODUCTION

Two-thirds of the earth is surrounded by water and appears blue (the planet of water) from space (UNEP, 1994). Lakes and rivers, the most important freshwater resources, account for 2.53% of the total water found on earth. Of the total water in the hydrosphere (4×10^8 cubic kilometers), 97.5% is deposited in the oceans that cover 71% of the earth's surface. Wetlands are estimated to occupy nearly 6.4% of the earth's surface – 30% bogs, 26% fens, 20% swamps, about 15% flood plains, etc. (IUCN, 1990). The amount of freshwater on earth is very small compared to seawater, of which 69.6% is locked away in the continental ice, 30.1% in underground aquifers, and 0.26% in rivers and lakes. Lakes, in particular, occupy less than 0.007% of the world's freshwater (UNEP, 1994). Wetlands, with a share of 0.0001% , among the global water sources, include swamps, marshes, bogs, and similar areas and are an important and vital component of the ecosystem (IUCN, 1990).

Wetlands play an important role in improving water quality by filtering sediments and nutrients from surface water. Aquatic vegetation helps in removing 90% of the dissolved nutrients like nitrogen and phosphorus and also in adsorption of heavy metals (Nixon and Lee, 1986).

The major cities of India are under the pressure of water scarcity. Chennai is among the worst affected because of its ever-expanding urban population demands for more freshwater. The availability and quality of water always have played an important role in determining the quality of life. Water quality is closely linked to water use and to the state of economic development. Freshwater habitats occupy a relatively small portion of the earth's surface when compared to marine and terrestrial habitats. Most of the pollutants mixed with water have led to a steady decline in aquatic life. Physical and chemical characteristics of water bodies affect the abundance, species composition, stability, productivity, and physiological condition of aquatic organisms. The physico-chemical parameters of an aquatic body not only reflect the type and diversity of aquatic biota but also the water quality (Hooper et al, 2005).

As we have discussed in the earlier chapters, population growth and rising income have resulted in a rapid growth in the MSW generation rate of the city. Waste generation per day has been doubled during the last decade. MSW generated in Chennai includes 68% of residential waste, 16% commercial waste, 14% institutional waste, and 2% industrial waste (Essaku et al 2007). The physico-chemical properties of the MSW generated in Chennai showed that the majority of the waste is composed of green waste (32.3%) and inert materials

(34.7%) viz., stones and glass (CPCB, 2000). It is also discussed that the area under the Perungudi dump yard in the Pallikaranai Marsh, south of Chennai, has increased tremendously between the years 1990 to 2010.

The dumping of municipal waste in the Perungudi dump yard is in operation since 1986 at Perungudi. This dump yard is a low-lying area and closes to the sea level. It is poorly drained and consists of an extensive area of marshy land, permanently wet and seasonally inundated. The current dumping rate is about 2,000 tons/day. The total area of this site is about 800 acres of which about 400 acres have been used so far for dumping. The dumpyard lies at 12°57'13.5" North and 80°14'5.8" East. (Karthikeyan et al, 2011). This dump yard does not have a proper lining to prevent leachate migration into the underlying and surrounding groundwater environment. There is no importance given for the measurement of potential impacts of leachate generation from the dump yard on groundwater quality. Hence, the present work is undertaken to study the nature of groundwater around the Perungudi dump yard by analyzing the physico-chemical characteristics, COD, BOD, and heavy metals (Figure 5.1).

Different types of vehicles deliver the waste to the dump yard resulting in a wide range of unloading procedures like end tipping, side tipping, and manual unloading. Unloaded waste is tipped into conical piles and then spread out by bulldozers. No cover of any description is placed over the spread waste to inhibit the ingress of surface water or to minimize litter blow and odor or to reduce the presence of vermin and insects. Since there are no specific arrangements to prevent the flow of water into and out of landfill sites, the diffusion of contaminants released during degradation of landfilled wastes may proceed uninhibited. The refuse is dumped in low-lying areas haphazardly, and as a result, the adjoining land gets enriched in salts and trace metals. Dumped waste comes in contact with water, causing pollution depending upon environmental conditions and solubility of metals.

▲ **Figure 5.1:**   Perungudi Dump Yard in Pallikaranai Marsh

To determine the quality of groundwater around the MSW disposal site in Pallikaranai and its adjacent area, a network of thirteen dug wells, nine tube wells, and four surface water sources was established as sample wells. The quality of water for the pre-monsoon and post-monsoon periods from June 2008. January 2009, June 2009, and January 2010 were determined and comparisons made with the water quality standards. Samples were collected to compare the COD, BOD, and heavy metals in the water samples in six observation wells in the same location both in dug wells and tube wells for the pre- and post-monsoon periods from June 2008 to January 2010.

ENVIRONMENTAL PROBLEMS DUE TO THE DUMP YARD

Other than the surface and groundwater pollution, the dump yard can cause air pollution. The natural decay of organic waste is associated with emissions of methane and hydrogen sulfide. Apart from waste delivering vehicle emissions, particulate matter and smoke derived from activities in the dump yard are very significant. Dust is raised from the passage of waste carrying vehicles over the un-medalled side roads, from the tipping and deposition of waste, from bulldozing activities spreading and compacting tipped waste. Depending upon the prevailing wind directions, the dust is blown off-site and deposited in areas beyond the site limits. In addition to the dust, the existing dump yard is subjected to a significant number of fires initiated by rag pickers on site as a means of liberating and recovering metals and non-combustible material from the waste. The lorries/trucks delivering waste affect the free flow of traffic and transport. Diseases can be caused by the dump yard to the local community through vectors, water, and air. Loss of flora and fauna habitats has also been observed (Figure 5. 2).

WASTE AT THE DUMPYARD

SEWAGE WATER LOGGING
ADJECENT TO DUMPYARD

TRESPASSING THROUGH DUMPYARD

WATER LOGGING IN DUMPYARD

WATER-LOGGING IN DUMPYARD

FIRE IN DUMPYARD

▲ **Figure 5.2:** Issues in Perungudi in Pallikaranai Marsh

The Perungudi dump yard is not fully secured by boundary walls on all sides, leading to the spreading of the dumped waste to nearby localities. Generally, the impacts of a dump yard may be summarized as follows:

- Groundwater contamination by the leachate generated by the waste dump
- Surface water contamination by the run-off from the waste dump
- Bad odor, pests, rodents, and wind-blown litter in and around the waste dump
- Generation of inflammable gases (e.g. methane) within the waste dump
- Bird menace above the waste dump that affects the flight of aircraft
- Fires within the waste dump
- Erosion and stability problems relating to slopes of the waste dump
- Epidemics through stray animals
- Acidity to the surrounding soil

Vencatesan (2007), reviewed issues related to the shrinkage of Pallikaranai Wetland. It was stated that the degradation of the marsh was due to the dumping of garbage and the disposal of partially treated sewage. The water quality analysis within the marsh and the adjoining water bodies showed the presence of mercury, lead, and cadmium was exceeding the permissible limit.

STUDY AREA AND METHODOLOGY

The Pallikaranai dump yard is located south of Velachery and lies between the Old Mahabalipuram Road in the east, Velachery–Tambaram road on the west, Sittalappakkam on the south, and Alandur on the north. It is a large topographic depression termed as the Pallikaranai depression, stretching approximately 10 km from north to south and is about to 3 km wide from west to east (Figure 5.1). The area is low-lying marshy land and is connected to the sea via the Buckingham Canal and the Kovalam Estuary at the southern end of the depression. The dump yard lies between 2 and 3 km west of the Buckingham Canal and is at 3.5 to 4.5 km west of the Bay of Bengal coastline. The locations of the dug wells, tube wells, and some surface waters are the sample well locations of the Central Ground Water Board, Chennai. With the prior permission of Central Ground Water Board, Chennai, the following locations were chosen for this study, which are within 2 km of the Perungudi dump yard. The locations were identified using the Global Positioning System (GPS) and the latitude and longitude values were recorded.

The groundwater occurs under an unconfined condition in alluvium and shallow weathered aquifer and under unconfined to confined conditions in deeper fracture aquifer. In general, the alluvial aquifers are developed through a dug well and shallow tube well. While the dug and borewells are used for groundwater development in the crystalline area (CGWB, Report, 2010).

In order to monitor the seasonal change in water level and water quality, thirteen dug wells, nine tube wells, and four surface water samples were established as sample wells. Groundwater samples were collected in two seasons of pre-monsoon and post-monsoon for a period of two years (June 2008 to January 2010) from thirteen dug wells, nine tube wells, and four surface water samples from Pallikaranai Marsh and Okkiyam Madugu were collected surrounding the dumping yard. Locations of the wells are given in (Table 5.1 and Figure 5.3).

For heavy metal analysis, separate samples were collected; after the collection of the water samples, the samples were acidified immediately with 1:1 Hydrochloric acid. Similarly, separate samples were collected for BOD and COD analysis. The samples were immediately transported to the laboratory and carefully stored for analysis in the TWAD Board, Chennai.

▼ **Table 5.1:** Locations of the Wells in the Study Area

Location	Latitude	Longitude	Well type
Pallikaranai Panchayat	12.9314	80.1978	dug well
Pallikaranai-New colony	12.9336	80.2069	dug well
Pallikaranai-Indira Nagar	12.9317	80.2092	Dug well
Perungudi-Elumalai-house	12.9556	80.2403	dug well
Perungudi-Thirumalainagar	12.9514	80.2272	dug well
Thuraipakkam	12.9514	80.2283	dug well
Thuraipakkam-shanmugam-house	12.9497	80.2267	dug well
Thuraipakkam-Adiparasakthi k. m	12.9619	80.2286	dug well
Thuraipakkam-Jayabalan-house	12.9500	80.2267	dug well
Thuraipakkam-Balamurugan garden	12.9397	80.2242	dug well
Thuraipakkam-PTC quarters	12.9586	80.2439	dug well
Mettukuppam Pillaiyar Koil street	12.9372	80.2217	dug well
Opp-balaji dental college	12.9411	80.2006	dug well
Pallikaranai-lake	12.9297	80.2050	surface water
Perungudi-lake (100ft road)	12.9511	80.2278	surface water
Thuraipakkam-near-LF	12.9500	80.2267	surface water
Okkiyam madhagu	12.9228	80.2325	surface water
Perungudi-Ramappa Nagar	12.9592	80.2272	tube well
Perungudi-Premvilla apts	12.9522	80.2263	tube well
Perungudi-Thirumalainagar	12.9514	80.2272	tube well
Perungudi-Elumalai-house	12.9556	80.2403	tube well
Thuraipakkam-shanmugam-house	12.9497	80.2267	tube well
Thuraipakkam-Adiparasakthi k. m	12.9619	80.2286	tube well
Thuraipakkam-Deenan house	12.9500	80.2267	tube well
Thuraipakkam-Jayabalan-house	12.9500	80.2267	tube well
Mettukuppam Pillaiyar Koil street	12.9372	80.2217	tube well

The samples were analyzed for relevant physico-chemical parameters such as pH, total dissolved solids, electrical conductivity, total hardness, calcium, magnesium, sodium, potassium, BOD, COD, carbonate, bicarbonate, chloride, fluoride, nitrate, sulfate, and heavy metals like iron, copper, cadmium, zinc, manganese, chromium, nickel and lead. pH & EC was measured in the field immediately after the collection of water samples. All the parameters were analyzed following the procedure specified in APHA (1998).

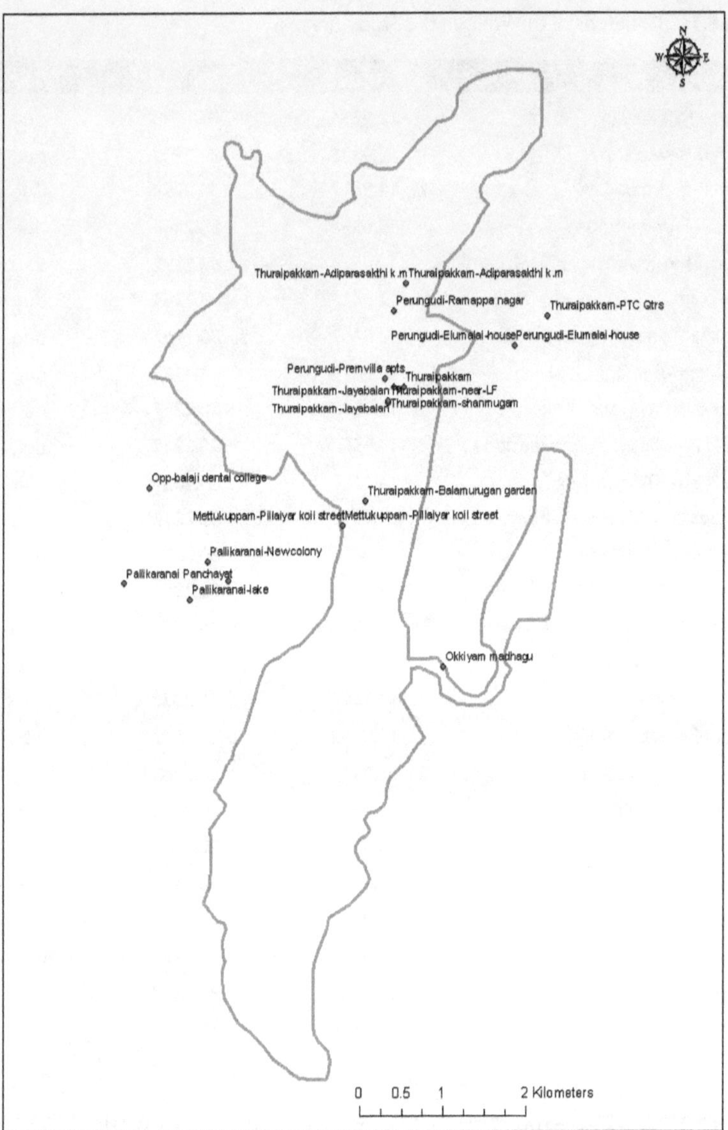

▲ **Figure 5.3:** Location of the Sample Wells in Pallikaranai Marsh

pH, EC, sodium, potassium, nitrate, sulfate, chloride, and fluoride were analyzed in the instrumental method. Total hardness, calcium, magnesium, carbonate, and bicarbonate were analyzed in the titrimetric method. All the heavy metals were analyzed with the atomic absorption spectrophotometric method. In the study area, the groundwater is used for domestic and other purposes. Analytical results for detailed chemical analysis, heavy metal analysis, BOD, and COD analysis are provided in Tables 5.2 and 5.3. All the samples were analyzed at the Water Analysis Laboratory in TWAD (Tamil Nadu Water Supply and Drainage Board), Chennai.

WATER QUALITY CHARACTERISTICS IN PALLIKARANAI MARSH

Water pollution is defined as the presence of impurities in such quantity and of nature as to impair the use of water for a stated purpose. When pollutants enter the water bodies, they get dissolved or lie suspended in water or get deposited on the bed. The water body is able to withstand the pollutants up to a certain threshold, beyond which the quality of water deteriorates. The various physico-chemical parameters for different seasons were evaluated and critically analyzed.

The average range of constituents during the pre-monsoon period of June 2008 and June 2009 and the average range of constituents during the post-monsoon period of January 2008 and January 2009 are discussed below.

Hydrogen Ion Concentration (pH)

The pH of water is very important and provides an important piece of information in many types of geochemical equilibrium or solubility calculations (Hem, 1985).

▼ **Table 5.2:** Average Range of Physico-chemical Parameters in Water During the Pre-monsoon Period (June 2008 and June 2009)

	Dug Well		Tube Well		Surface Water	
	Min	Max	Min	Max	Min	Max
pH	6.75	8.12	7.08	7.89	7.230	7.580
EC (Microsiemen/cm at 25°)	1334	4853	1199	7254	536	3237
TDS (Total dissolved solids) (mg/l)	1535	6053	1164	6488	645	4596
Chlorides (mg/l)	216	1356	97	1466	230	2285
Fluoride (mg/l)	0.33	0.79	0.29	0.71	0.23	1.71

	Dug Well		Tube Well		Surface Water	
	Min	Max	Min	Max	Min	Max
Total Hardness in CaCO₃ (mg/l)	1267	331	1273	141	1249	177
Calcium (mg/l)	37	237	22	100	33	68
Magnesium (mg/l)	36	141	18	331	25	260
Nitrate (mg/l)	157	886	18	1362	954	59
Potassium	8	187	9	203	13	153
Bicarbonate (mg/l)	140	1747	178	1744	148	618
Nitrates (mg/l)	13.20	421.80	37.60	311.20	9.82	145.60
Sodium (mg/l)	53	617	26	969	74	520
Copper (mg/l)	0.01	0.02	0.01	0.06	BDL	0.01
Lead (mg/l)	0.02	0.10	0.02	0.05	0.02	0.09
Zinc (mg/l)	0.01	0.67	0.06	0.37	0.01	0.07
Nickel (mg/l)	0.01	0.08	0.01	0.08	BDL	0.03
Cadmium (mg/l)	BDL	BDL	BDL	BDL	BDL	BDL
Chromium (mg/l)	BDL	0.23	BDL	0.02	BDL	0.01
Manganese (mg/l)	0.01	1.64	0.04	0.68	0.01	0.71
Iron (mg/l)	0.03	0.18	0.05	0.37	0.09	0.02
COD (mg/l)	206	276	82	269	20.	117
BOD (mg/l)	88	155	86	127	6.2	40

Source: Based on the data compiled and analyzed by the Author

▼ **Table 5.3:** Average Range of Physico-chemical Parameters in Water During the Post-monsoon Period (January 2008 and January 2009)

	Dug Well		Tube Well		Surface Water	
	Min	Max	Min	Max	Min	Max
pH	6.98	7.64	6.80	7.79	7.28	7.54
EC (Microsiemen/cm at 25⁰)	1020	4090	1161	4406	632	6102
TDS (Total dissolved solids) (mg/l)	1316	7859	1148	4573	697	5306
Chlorides (mg/l)	1404	1792	124	1017	119	1531
Fluoride (mg/l)	1.31	0.64	0.60	1.51	0.59	1.05
Total Hardness in CaCO₃ (mg/l)	1120	225	250	632	42	420
Calcium (mg/l)	61	386	27	140	26	94
Magnesium (mg/l)	23	168	9	107	13	98
Nitrate (mg/l)	24	1355	54	1270	150	941
Potassium	6	182	5	28	6	49
Bicarbonate (mg/l)	137	1290	143	1213	171	833

	Dug Well		Tube Well		Surface Water	
	Min	Max	Min	Max	Min	Max
Nitrates (mg/l)	5.97	347.70	6.75	177.84	6.20	129.72
Sodium (mg/l)	41	1018	70	633	26	482
Copper (mg/l)	BDL	0.26	BDL	0.55	BDL	0.02
Lead (mg/l)	BDL	0.10	0.02	0.11	0.02	0.08
Zinc (mg/l)	0.03	0.11	BDL	0.28	0.02	0.06
Nickel (mg/l)	BDL	0.33	BDL	0.38	0.01	0.07
Cadmium (mg/l)	BDL	0.01	BDL	0.11	BDL	BDL
Chromium (mg/l)	BDL	0.01	BDL	0.01	BDL	0.02
Manganese (mg/l)	BDL	1.79	0.01	1.80	0.01	0.54
Iron (mg/l)	0.03	2.49	0.01	1.02	0.09	0.66
COD (mg/l)	93	129	31	119	25	129
BOD (mg/l)	23	88	31	127	5.8	92.0

Source: Based on the data compiled and analyzed by the Author

The pH is one of the most important operational water quality parameters as it influences many chemical and biological processes within a water body. The pH values range from 0-14 (i. e. very acidic to very alkaline). pH < 7 indicates an acidic solution (i. e. H^+ ions exceed the OH^- ions). However, pH >7 indicates an alkaline solution (i. e. OH^- ions and H^+ ions). pH equal to seven shows a neutral condition where H^+ and OH^- ions have the same concentrations. The balance between carbon dioxide, carbonate, and bicarbonate ions is most often controlled by the pH of natural water (Fletcher, 1986). In as much as the solubility of carbon dioxide changes with pressure and temperature, so temperature plays an important role in determining the pH. High pH values (>8.5) are commonly associated with sodium carbonate–bicarbonates. Moderately high pH values with waters high in bicarbonates and low values (<4.0) are associated with water containing free acids derived from oxidizing sulfide minerals. Most of the aquatic flora is flourished within the pH value of either side of seven. Rapidly growing algae or submerged aquatic vegetation removes CO_2 from the water during photosynthesis, significantly increasing pH levels. On perusal of the table, the pH of the dug wells, tube wells, and surface water varies from 6.75 to 8.12. This shows that the pH is alkaline in nature in the water samples (Table 5.4.1, Figure 5.4.1).

During the post-monsoon period, the pH varies from 6.98 to 7.79 and is alkaline in nature in all water samples of dug wells, tube wells, and surface water. Thus, the alkaline pH is particularly due to bicarbonates. On comparison of pH ranges in different periods like the pre- and post-monsoon, notable changes are not seen.

The limit of pH value for drinking water is specified as 6.5 to 8. On analysis, it is seen that there are variations in the range of pH values in the study area for a different time period. This reveals that the pH values are in a decreasing trend from more alkaline to neutral with respect to time in the study area. Fresh input of water from precipitation may be responsible for the changes that have taken place in the study area. Alkaline water may decrease the solubility of metals. The alkalinity varies in accordance with the fluctuation in the pollution load (Jinwal and Dixit, 2008). The pH affects taste and corrodes the water supply system (CGWB Report, 2004).

Electrical Conductivity (Microsiemen/cm at 25°C)

Specific electrical conductance is a measure of the ability of a substance to conduct an electrical current. It is the reciprocal of the resistance in ohms of a column of solution one centimeter at a specified temperature, usually at 25° C.

The electrical conductivity (EC) has a direct relation with the total solids. High conductivity leads to a high amount of dissolved ions such as sodium, calcium, magnesium, chlorides, sulfates, bicarbonates, and carbonates in water. In the present study, the EC in the pre-monsoon period varies from 536 to 7254μS /cm and in the post-monsoon period the EC varies from 632 to 6102 μS /cm. During the post-monsoon season, there is a reduction in EC in the dug wells, and tube wells, whereas for the surface water an increase is noticed. The EC value for sediment contaminated by waste landfills was found to be in the range of 120- 622 μS/cm (Ramanand Narayanan, 2008) (Table 5.4.2, Figure 5.4.2).

▼ **Table 5.4.1:**   Average pH Content During Pre-monsoon and Post-monsoon Period

Well Type	Pre-monsoon	Post-monsoon
Dug well	7.58	7.31
Tube well	7.48	7.18
Surface water	7.40	7.34

pH: maximum allowable limit 6.5 to 9.2 (CPHEEO, 1999)

▼ **Table 5.4.2:**   Average EC Content During Pre-monsoon and Post-monsoon Period

Well Type	Pre-monsoon	Post-monsoon
Dug well	3234	2459
Tube well	3775	2950
Surface water	1887	1742

EC: Not applicable. (CPHEEO, 1999)

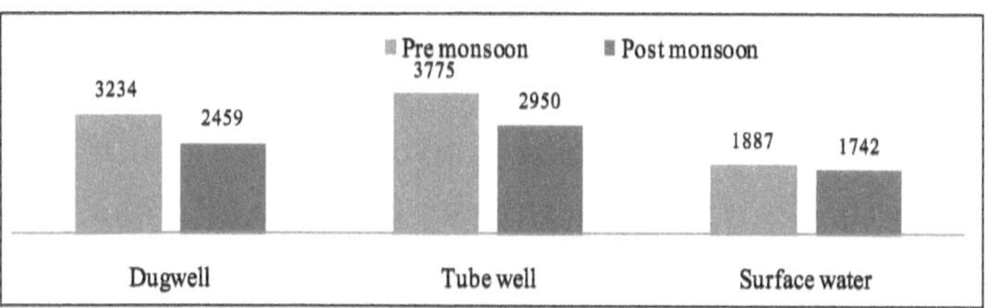

▲ **Figure 5.4.2:**   Average EC Content During Pre-monsoon and Post-monsoon Period

Total Dissolved Solids (TDS)

Total dissolved solids (TDS) indicates the general nature of the water quality or salinity and measures the total concentration of all constituents present in the water. TDS comprises inorganic salts (principally calcium, magnesium, potassium, sodium, bicarbonates, chlorides, and sulfates) and small amounts of organic matter that are dissolved in water. These determine the flow of water in and out of the cells of organisms and are essential at certain levels to maintain aquatic life. High TDS content leads to eutrophication. All species of fish and other aquatic life must tolerate a range of dissolved solids concentrations in order to survive under natural conditions.

The present study reveals that the TDS in the pre-monsoon period varies from 697mg/l to 5306 mg/l with an average of 3162 mg/l in dug wells, 4114 mg/l in tube wells, and 2821 mg/l in surface water. During the post-monsoon period, it varies from 645 to 6488 mg/l with an average of 2621 mg/l in dug wells, 2972mg/l in tube wells, and 2460 mg/l in surface water. This reveals that data is exceeding the limit prescribed in the CPHEEO (1999) maximum allowable limit of 2000mg/l. We must keep in mind that in areas like this, some of the values observed may be site-specific due to local conditions (Table 5.4.3).

▼ **Table 5.4.3:** Average TDS Content During Pre-monsoon and Post-monsoon Period

Well Type	Pre-monsoon	Post-monsoon
Dug well	3162	2621
Tube well	4114	2972
Surface water	1781	1902

TDS: the maximum desirable limit is 2000 (CPHEEO, 1999)

The high level of TDS is due to natural sources, sewage, and urban run-off. A large amount of total solids makes the water body more turbid and increases its electrical conductivity (Hasan and Rajia, 2009). Also, the palatability decreases and it may cause gastrointestinal irritation in humans (CGWB Report, 2004).

▼ **Table 5.4.4:** Average Total Hardness as Calcium Carbonate Content During Pre-monsoon and Post-monsoon Period

Well Type	Pre-monsoon	Post-monsoon
Dug well	627	452
Tube well	564	391
Surface water	648	306

Maximum allowable: 600 mg/l & desirable limit is 200mg/l. (CPHEEO, 1999)

Total Hardness

According to the classification of Dufor and Becker (1964), for total hardness, the groundwater of the area comes under the classification very hard as the calcium and magnesium are high and are the important parameters for measuring the total hardness. Hardness is an important criterion for determining the usability of water for domestic, drinking, and many industrial supplies (Karanath, 1987).

During the pre-monsoon period, the total hardness is generally high in dug wells, tube wells, and surface water (varies from 141 to 1249) than the post-monsoon period (varies from 42 to 1120). According to CPHEEO, (1999) the maximum allowable is 600 mg/l and the desirable limit is 200mg/l for total hardness. In the pre-monsoon period, the total hardness values in the present study exceed the CPHEEO, (1999) the maximum allowable of 600 mg/l, and post-monsoon period the values exceed the CPHEEO, (1999) desirable limit of 200mg/l (Table 5.4.4, Figure 5.4.4). An increase in total hardness values affects the water supply system (scaling), causes excessive soap consumption, calcification of arteries, and may cause urinary concretions, diseases of kidney or bladder, and stomach disorders (CGWB Report, 2004).

Calcium

The calcium content varies from 9-386 mg/l in the pre-monsoon periods for the dug wells, tube wells, and surface water. Similarly, it varies between 22-237 mg/l in the post-monsoon period. The CPHEEO (1999) desirable limit for calcium is 75mg/l. In the pre-monsoon periods, the average value exceeds the desirable limit and in the post-monsoon period other than the average calcium content in the tube well, the rest exceeds the desirable limit (Table 5.4.5, Figure 5.4.5). Excess of calcium content in water causes concretions in the body such as kidney or bladder stones and irritation in urinary passages (CGWB Report, 2004).

▼ **Table 5.4.5:** Average Calcium Content During Pre-monsoon and Post-monsoon Period

Well Type	Pre-monsoon	Post-monsoon
Dug well	136	88
Tube well	77	48
Surface water	66	53

Desirable limits for calcium:75mg/l. (CPHEEO, 1999)

Sulfate

The concentration of sulfate in the water samples during the pre-monsoon period varies from 26-069 mg/l and in the post-monsoon period varies from 26-1018 mg/l. The average concentration of sulfate in the pre-monsoon periods is above the desirable limit of the standard of CPHEEO, (1999) i.e., 200 mg/l except for surface water sample during the post-monsoon period which is just with the standard limit. This may be due to rains (Table 5.4.10, Figure 5.4.10). High concentrations of sulfate cause gastrointestinal irritation and with magnesium or sodium can have a cathartic effect on users (CGWB Report, 2004).

▼ **Table 5.4.10:** Average Sulfate Content During Pre-monsoon and Post-monsoon Period

Well Type	Pre-monsoon	Post-monsoon
Dug well	257	236
Tube well	362	290
Surface water	295	172

The desirable limit for sulfates:200mg/l (CPHEEO, 1999)

Chloride

The chloride content during the pre-monsoon period for groundwater and surface water varied from 97-2285 mg/l and in the post-monsoon period, it varied from 119-1531 mg/l. The average chloride content in the present study during the pre-monsoon and post-monsoon periods for dug wells, tube wells, and surface water were exceeding the desirable limit for drinking water (200 mg/l) (CPHEEO, 1999). In the locations closer to the dump yard, the values exceeded the maximum allowable limit of 1000 mg/l. (CPHEEO, 1999) (Table 5.4.11, Figure 5.4.11). Chloride is important in detecting the concentration of groundwater by wastewater. A high concentration of chloride is considered to be the indicators of pollution due to organic wastes of animal or industrial origin. Chloride also gets added to waters from the discharge of industrial effluents or contamination with sewage (Kumar et al, 2011).

▼ **Table 5.4.11:**   Average Chloride Content During Pre-monsoon and Post-monsoon Period

Well Type	Pre-monsoon	Post-monsoon
Dug well	731	432
Tube well	956	650
Surface water	679	616

The desirable limit for chloride: 200mg/l (CPHEEO, 1999)

Fluoride

The fluoride content varied from 0.23 to 1.71 mg/l during the pre-monsoon period and 0.60 to 1.51 mg/l during the post-monsoon period. The fluoride content during the post-monsoon period exceeded the desirable of 1 mg/l by CPHEE (1999), in small pockets closer to the Perungudi dump yard, both in the pre-monsoon and post-monsoon periods (Table 5.4.12, Figure 5.4.12). A very high concentration of fluoride may cause crippling skeletal fluorosis (CGWB Report, 2004).

▼ **Table 5.4.12:**   Average Fluoride Content During Pre-monsoon and Post-monsoon Period

Well Type	Pre-monsoon	Post-monsoon
Dug well	1	1
Tube well	0	1
Surface water	1	1

The desirable limit for fluoride:1 mg/l (CPHEEO, 1999)

Nitrate

Nitrate is one of the major indicators of anthropogenic sources of pollution. The nitrate in groundwater is contributed from atmospheric precipitation, industrial sources, sewage source, run-off from agriculture fields, and leachates from landfill sites (Lee et al. 2003; Jalali 2005). The contribution from the atmospheric is minimal. The major sources of nitrate are related to the activities of humans. Nitrate is the ultimate oxidized product of all nitrogen-containing and its occurrence in groundwater can be fairly attributed to the infiltration of fertilizer and industrial pollution.

The nitrate content during the pre-monsoon period for the groundwater and surface water varied from 9.82 to 421.80 mg/l and in the post-monsoon period varied from 5.97 to 177.84 mg/l.

The average nitrate value during the pre-monsoon and post-monsoon in dug wells, tube wells, and surface water exceeded the CPHEEO (1999) standard of 45 mg/l (Table 5.4.13, Figure 5.4.13). High nitrate content causes infant methemoglobinemia (Blue Babies) at very high concentrations, causes gastric cancer, and adversely affects the central nervous system and cardiovascular system (CGWB Report, 2004).

▼ **Table 5.4.13:** Average Nitrate Content During Pre-Monsoon and Post-Monsoon Period

Well Type	Pre-monsoon	Post-monsoon
Dug well	107	74
Tube well	171	86
Surface water	94	59

The desirable limit for nitrate:45 mg/l (CPHEEO, 1999)

COD

Chemical Oxygen Demand (COD) is a measure of oxygen equivalent to the organic matter content of the water susceptible to oxidation by a strong chemical oxidant and thus is an index of organic pollution. A COD test measures all organic carbon with the exception in the case of certain aromatics, which are not completely oxidized in the reaction. COD indicates the pollution level in a water body as it is related to the organic matter present in it (Panigrahi, 2007).

The COD value varies from 20 to 276 mg/l in the pre-monsoon period and 25 to 129 mg/l during the post-monsoon period. The COD is high in the pre-monsoon season and exceeds the limits prescribed in the Indian Standard 250 mg/l which is the indication of the organic contaminants in the water body. The COD content is less in the post-monsoon period probably due to the rainy season (Hasan and Rajia, 2009). Drinking water should not have oxygen demand and so COD should be Nil (CPHEEO, 1999) (Table 5.4.14, Figure 5.4.14).

▼ **Table 5.4.14:** Average Cod Content During Pre-monsoon and Post-monsoon Period

Well Type	Pre-monsoon	Post-monsoon
Dug Well	37.27	36.73
Tube Well	38.39	35.83
Surface Water	21	18.50

BOD (Biological Oxygen Demand)

Biological oxygen demand (BOD) is a chemical procedure for determining the amount of dissolved oxygen needed by aerobic biological organisms in a body of water to break down organic matter present, at a certain temperature, over a specific period of time. All organic materials or waste can be broken down or decomposed by microbial and other biological activities. Most organic compounds that exhibit BOD is because oxygen is used in the degradation process. Therefore, the more the organic matter, the higher the BOD level.

In the present study, BOD values vary from 6.2 to 155 mg/l in the pre-monsoon period for dug wells, tube wells, and surface water. The BOD is lower in the post-monsoon season and varies from 5.8 to 127 mg/l. In the surface water during the post-monsoon season, BOD is the least. The average BOD was high in the case of dug wells, tube wells, and surface water both in the pre-monsoon and post-monsoon periods.

During the post-monsoon season, the BOD reduced, from which it is clear that during the rainy season the water gets diluted (Hasan and Rajia, 2009). The increase in BOD during the pre-monsoon period is due to the dumping of household garbage and improper dumping of MSW in the Perungudi dump yard (Table 5.4.15, Figure 5.4.15)

▼ **Table 5.4.15:** Average Bod Content During Pre-monsoon and Post-monsoon Period

Well Type	Pre-monsoon	Post-monsoon
Dug Well	14.47	8.30
Tube Well	8.59	5.56
Surface Water	33.75	5.60

HEAVY METALS IN WATER IN PALLIKARANAI MARSH

The toxic heavy metals entering the ecosystem may lead to geo-accumulation, bioaccumulation, and bio-magnification. Heavy metals like Fe, Cu, Zn, Ni, Cr, Pb, Cd, and other trace elements are important for the proper functioning of biological systems and their deficiency or excess could lead to a number of disorders. Food chain contamination by heavy metals has potential accumulation in bio-systems through contaminated water, soil, and air. Most of our water resources are gradually becoming polluted due to the addition of foreign materials from the surroundings (Lokeswari and Chandrappa, 2006).

In the present study, it was found that the minimum and maximum content of heavy metals in the pre- and post-monsoon seasons from June 2008 to January 2010 in all wells were copper (BDL-0.55mg/l), iron (0.01-2.49 mg/l), zinc (BDL-0.67mg/l), lead (BDL-0.10mg/l), nickel, (BDL-0.38mg/l), manganese (BDL-0.86mg/l), chromium (BDL-0.023 mg/l) and cadmium (BDL-0.11mg/l).

Here, we will be discussing the average heavy metal content in the dug wells, tube wells, and surface water in both pre- and post-monsoon periods.

The average copper content was 0.06mg/l, which exceeded the desirable of CPHEEO (1999) (0.05mg/l) in the pre-monsoon periods and the values are high in the well locations which are closer to the dump yard (Table 5.5.1, Figure 5.5.1). A large amount of copper content in water may result in liver damage, cause CNS irritation, and depression. In the water supply system, it enhances the corrosion of aluminum particular (CGWB report, 2004).

The average iron content was 0.35 mg/l in the dug wells, tube wells, and surface water in both pre- and post-monsoon periods which exceeded the CPHEEO (1999) desirable value of 0.10 mg/l. The iron content was higher in the post-monsoon season (Table 5.5.2, Figure 5.5.2). High content of iron has an adverse effect on domestic uses and water supply structures (IS 10500, BIS, 2003).

▼ **Table 5.5.1:** Average Copper Content During Pre-monsoon and Post-monsoon Period

Well Type	Pre-monsoon	Post-monsoon
Dug well	0.0031	0.02
Tube well	0.02	0.02
Surface water	0.005	0.01

Desirable limit for copper: 0.05 mg/l (CPHEEO, 1999)

▼ **Table 5.5.2:** Average Iron Content During Pre-monsoon and Post-monsoon Period

Well Type	Pre-monsoon	Post-monsoon
Dug well	0.14	0.3
Tube well	0.16	0.25
Surface water	0.32	0.56

Desirable limit for iron:0.1 mg/l (CPHEEO, 1999)

In the case of zinc, the average value was 0.05mg/l in the dug wells, tube wells, and surface water in both the pre- and post-monsoon periods and was below the desirable limit of CPHEEO (1999), (5.00 mg/l) (Table 5.5.3, Figure 5.5.3). Zinc is an essential element in human metabolism. The taste threshold for zinc occurs at about 5 mg/l when it imparts astringent taste to water (CGWB Report, 2004).

▼ **Table 5.5.3:** Average Zinc Content During Pre-monsoon and Post-monsoon Period

Well Type	Pre-monsoon	Post-monsoon
Dug well	0.18	0.06
Tube well	0.22	0.08
Surface water	0.01	0.04

Desirable limit for zinc: 5 mg/l (CPHEEO, 1999)

The average lead content was 0.06mg/l in the dug wells, tube wells, and surface water in both pre- and post-monsoon periods and was above the desirable limit of CPHEEO (1999), (0.05 mg/l) (Table 5.5.4, Figure 5.5.4). Toxic in acute and chronic exposures of lead content in water leads to burning in the mouth, severe inflammation of gastrointestinal tract with vomiting and diarrhea, chronic toxicity produces nausea, severe abdominal pain, paralysis, mental confusion, visual disturbances, anemia, etc. (CGWB Report, 2004).

▼ **Table 5.5.4:** Average Lead Content During Pre-monsoon and Post-monsoon Period

Well Type	Pre-monsoon	Post-monsoon
Dug well	0.05	0.06
Tube well	0.05	0.07
Surface water	0.03	0.02

Desirable limit for lead: 0. 05 mg/l (CPHEEO, 1999)

Similarly, the average nickel content was 0.30mg/l in the dug wells, tube wells, and surface water in both pre and post-monsoon periods which exceed the drinking water (IS: 10500, 1991) value of 0000.10mg/l. The average nickel content was higher in the post-monsoon season (Table 5.5.5, Figure 5.5.5). This is due to the solubility and mobility of species within the landfill and also the influence of the pH value. High levels of nickel content may be carcinogenic (cancerous) and can react with DNA resulting in DNA damage (CGWB Report, 2004).

▼ **Table 5.5.5:** Average Nickel Content During Pre-monsoon and Post-monsoon Period

Well Type	Pre-monsoon	Post-monsoon
Dug well	0.03	0.03
Tube well	0.03	0.05
Surface water	0.02	0.04

Desirable limit for Nickel: 0. 10 mg/l (IS: 10500, 1991), (BIS, 2003)

The average manganese content was 0.32 mg/l in the dug wells, tube wells, and surface water in both pre and post-monsoon periods, which exceeded the desirable limits of CPHEEO, (1999) with a value of 0.05mg/l (Table 5.5.6, Figure 5.5.6). Beyond this limit, taste/appearance is affected and it has an adverse effect on domestic uses and water supply structures (IS 10500, BIS, 2003).

▼ **Table 5.5.6:** Average Manganese Content During Pre-monsoon and Post-monsoon Period

Well Type	Pre-monsoon	Post-monsoon
Dug well	0.42	0.5
Tube well	BDL*	BDL*
Surface water	0.06	0.07

*BDL; Below detectable limit
Desirable limit for manganese: 0. 05 mg/l (CPHEEO, 1999)

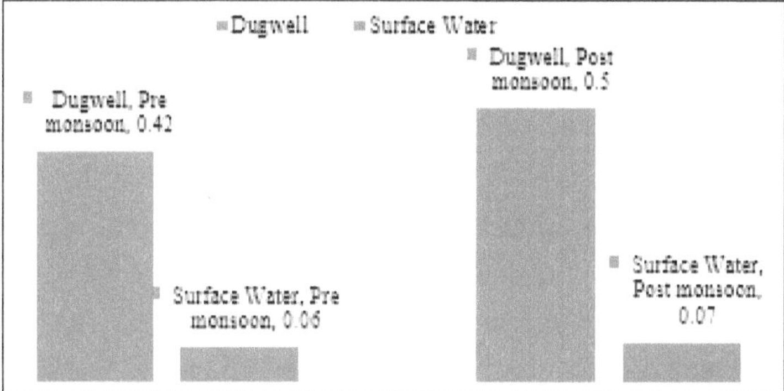

▲ **Figure 5.5.6:** Average Manganese Content During Pre-monsoon and Post-monsoon Period

High values of chromium content in water were seen in a few water samples that are closer to the dump yard in the locations of Perungudi-Thirumalainagar, Perungudi-Elumalai-house Thuraipakkam-Jayabalan, and Thuraipakkam-Balamurugan garden with an average value of 0.02mg/l and is within the desirable value of CPHEEO, (1999) (0.05mg/l) (Table 5.5.7, Figure 5.5.7). The hexavalent state of chromium produces lung tumors and can produce coetaneous and nasal mucous membrane ulcers and dermatitis (CGWB Report, 2004).

▼ **Table 5.5.7:** Average Chromium Content During Pre-monsoon and Post-monsoon Period

Well Type	Pre-monsoon	Post-monsoon
Dug well	0.02	0.004
Tube well	0.01	0.002
Surface Water	BDL*	BDL*

*BDL; Below detectable limit

Desirable limit for chromium: 0. 05 mg/l (CPHEEO, 1999)

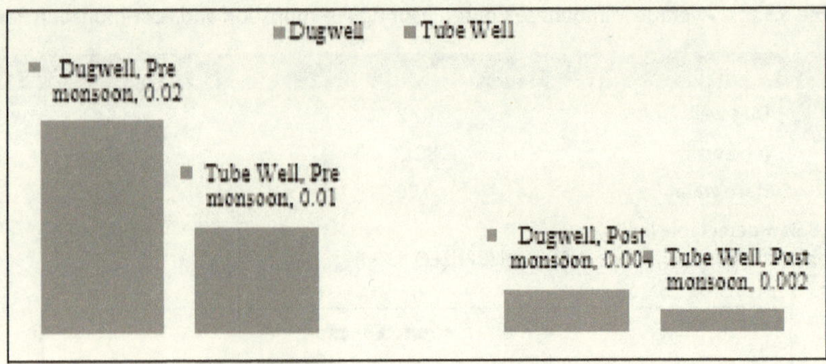

▲ **Figure 5.5.7:**   Average Chromium Content During Pre-monsoon and Post-monsoon Period

The cadmium content was seen in the water samples in four locations close to the dump yard and the average cadmium content was 0.01mg/l. This was from Thuraippakam-Jayabalan both in dug wells and tube wells and Thuraippakam-Shanmugam both in tube wells and dug wells. The desirable level for cadmium was 0.01mg/l by CPHEEO (1999), and the average cadmium content in the present study is within the desirable limit (Table 5.5.8, Figure 5.5.8). Acute toxicity may be associated with renal, arterial hypertension, itai-itai disease. Cadmium salts cause cramps, nausea, vomiting, and diarrhea (CGWB Report, 2004).

▼ **Table 5.5.8:**   Average Cadmium Content During Pre-monsoon and Post-monsoon Period

Well Type	Pre-monsoon	Post-monsoon
Dug well	0.01	BDL*
Tube well	0.01	BDL*
Surface water	BDL*	BDL*

*BDL; Below detectable limit
Desirable limit for cadmium: 0. 01 mg/l (CPHEEO, 1999)
Source: Based on the data compiled and analyzed by the Author

The extent of contamination of groundwater quality due to landfill waste depends upon a number of factors like leachate composition, rainfall, depth, and distance of the well from the pollution source. The contaminant concentrations tend to decrease during the post-monsoon seasons and increase during the pre-monsoon seasons in most of the samples due to the dilution effect. However, in the unprotected landfill sites, due to the migration of contaminants from the landfill site, post-monsoon values might be higher than the pre-monsoon values. Some of the samples near the landfill sites show higher in the post-monsoon period than the pre-monsoon. This is due to the migration effect of the contaminant.

The heavy metal concentration in the marsh showed significant variations from one sampling point to another. The maximum concentrations of heavy metals were found near the Perungudi dump yard. Garbage dumping and burning in the middle and along the roads causes severe pollution (Jayaprakash, 2010). The high value of heavy metal concentration is due to the dumping of waste from industrial, municipal, and domestic activities (Prabu, 2009). Elevated trace metal concentrations may lead to toxic effects or bio-magnification in the aquatic environment.

The extent of contamination of groundwater quality due to landfill waste depends upon a member of factors like leachate composition, rainfall, depth, and distance of the well from the pollution source. The contaminant concentrations tend to decrease during the post-monsoon season and increase during the pre-monsoon seasons in most of the samples due to the dilution effect. However, in the unprotected landfill sites, due to the migration of contaminants from landfill sites, sometimes the post-monsoon values might be higher than the pre-monsoon values. In some, the post-monsoon values are high near the landfill sites than the pre-monsoon due to the migration effect of contaminants. Temporal variation of the COD, BOD, and heavy metals in the groundwater from the six locations both for dug well and tube wells from June 2008 to January 2010 are presented (Tables 5.6 and 5.7, Figures 5.6 and 5.7). The location of the dug wells and tube wells are given below with respective abbreviations.

Location	Abbreviation
Perungudi-Elumalai-house	PG-E
Perungudi-Thirumalainagar	PG-T
Thuraipakkam-shanmugam	TP-S
Thuraipakkam-Adiparasakthi K. M.	TP-A
Thuraipakkam-Jayabalan	TP-J
Mettukuppam Pillaiyar Koil street	MP-PK

SEASONAL VARIATION IN COD VALUE IN DUG WELLS AND TUBE WELLS DURING JUNE 2008, JANUARY 2009, JUNE 2009 AND JANUARY 2010

The COD values in the dug wells during the pre-monsoon and post-monsoon periods in June 2008, January 2009, June 2008, and January 2010 show that the pre-monsoon values are higher than the post-monsoon values. The COD values in Thuraipakkam-Shanmugam and Perungudi-Elumalai House are high as they are close to the dump yard. Whereas, the values in the location Mettukuppam Pillaiyar Koil street is low as it away from the dump yard.

The COD values in the tube wells during the pre-monsoon and post-monsoon periods in June 2008, January 2009, June 2009, and January 2010 show that the pre-monsoon values are higher than the post-monsoon values. They are the highest in the location Thuraipakkam-Jayabalan and are closer to the dumpsite. The values in the location Mettukuppam Pillaiyar Koil street is low both in pre-monsoon and post-monsoon season as the location is away from the dump yard. A similar trend was seen in the dug wells values for COD (Table 5.6, Figure 5.6).

▼ **Table 5.6:** Seasonal Variations in COD Content in Water in Dug Wells and Tube Wells for the Period June 2008 – January 2010

Location	Well type	June-08	Jan-09	June-09	Jan-10
Perungudi-Elumalai-house	dugwell	255	121	245	117
Perungudi-Thirumalainagar	dugwell	269	127	261	120
Thuraipakkam-shanmugam-house	dugwell	276	123	279	121
Thuraipakkam-Adiparasakthi k. m	dugwell	252	117	257	123
Thuraipakkam-Jayabalan-house	dugwell	276	125	269	129
Mettukuppam Pillaiyarkoil street	dugwell	239	98	206	93
Perungudi-Elumalai-house	tube well	235	111	239	113
Perungudi-Thirumalainagar	tube well	259	107	251	100
Thuraipakkam-shanmugam-house	tube well	256	103	259	101
Thuraipakkam-Adiparasakthi k. m	tube well	252	95	247	92
Thuraipakkam-Jayabalan-house	tube well	266	115	269	119
Mettukuppam Pillaiyarkoil street	tube well	82	31	85	34

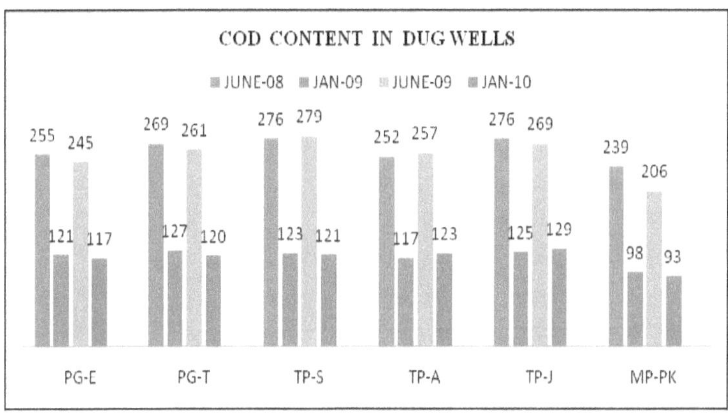

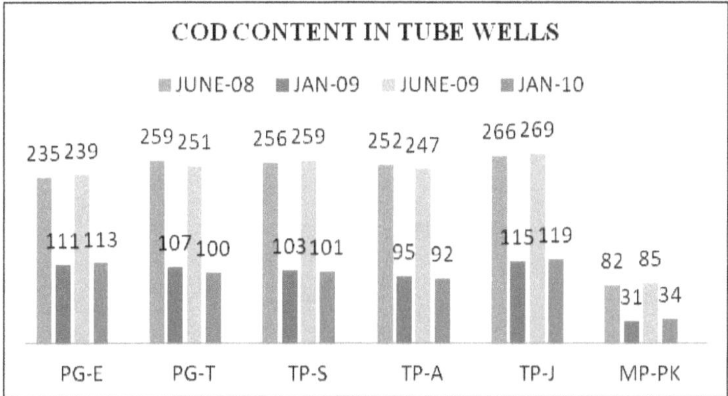

▲ **Figure 5.6:** Seasonal Variations in COD Content in Water in Dug Wells and Tube Wells for the Period June 2008-January 2010
Source: Based on the data compiled and analyzed by the author

SEASONAL VARIATION IN BOD VALUE IN DUG WELLS AND TUBE WELLS DURING JUNE 2008, JANUARY 2009, JUNE 2009 AND JANUARY 2010

The BOD values in the dug wells during the pre-monsoon and post-monsoon season show that the values are higher in the pre-monsoon periods than the post-monsoon period. The values in pre-monsoon and post-monsoon periods were high in all the locations closer to the dumpsite; except in Thuraipakkam-Adiparasakthi K. M. it is slightly low as it is a little away from the dumpsite and it is low in the location Mettukuppam Pillayar Koil street which is away from the dump yard (Table 5.7, Figure 5.7).

▼ **Table 5.7:** Seasonal Variation in BOD Content in Water in Dug Wells and Tube Wells for the Period June 2008 –January 2010

Location	Well type	June-08	Jan-09	June-09	Jan-10
Perungudi-Elumalai-house	dug well	132	45	135	29
Perungudi-Thirumalainagar	dug well	127	40	130	45
Thuraipakkam-shanmugam- house	dug well	135	35	138	45
Thuraipakkam-Adiparasakthi k. m	dug well	108	57	102	40
Thuraipakkam-Jayabalan- house	dug well	147	56	155	52
Mettukuppam Pillaiyar Koil street	dug well	88	23	95	88
Perungudi-Elumalai-house	tube well	117	46	127	49
Perungudi-Thirumalainagar	tube well	116	52	116	58
Thuraipakkam-shanmugam- house	tube well	88	30	88	43
Thuraipakkam-Adiparasakthi k. m	tube well	120	68	120	65
Thuraipakkam-Jayabalan- house	tube well	113	63	114	55
Mettukuppam Pillaiyar Koil street	tube well	86	34	98	31

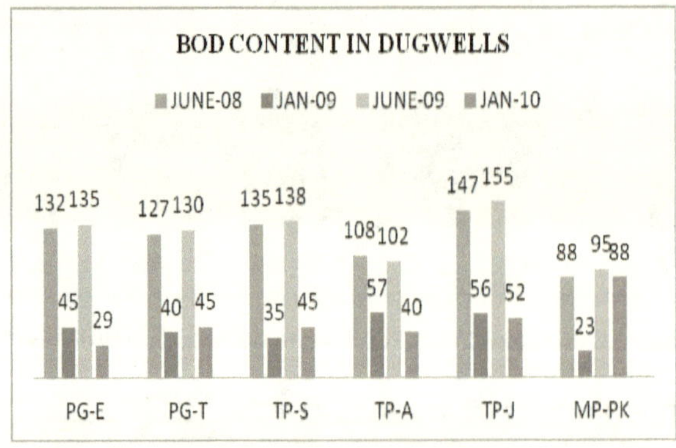

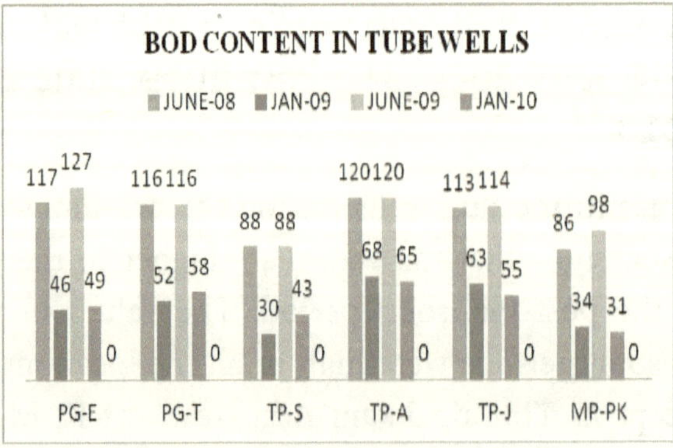

▲ **Figure 5.7:** Seasonal Variation in BOD Content in Water in Dug Wells and Tube Wells for the Period June 2008- January 2010

Source: Based on the data compiled and analyzed by the author

In the tube wells data for BOD, the trend is similar to the case of the dug wells. The BOD values in the tube wells during the pre-monsoon and post-monsoon studied during June 2008, January 2009, June 2009, and January 2010 show that the values are higher in the pre-monsoon period than the post-monsoon period.

As in the case of dug wells, the values in the pre-monsoon and post-monsoon periods were high in locations closer to the dump yard and the values in the locations of Mettukuppam-Pillayarkoil Street are low as it is away from the dump yard.

SEASONAL VARIATION OF HEAVY METALS IN GROUNDWATER FROM THE LOCATIONS BOTH IN DUG WELLS AND TUBE WELLS DURING THE PRE-MONSOON AND POST-MONSOON PERIOD (JUNE 2008-JANUARY 2010)

Copper (mg/l)

In Figure 5.8.1, it is seen that the average copper content in the water sample was high during the post-monsoon period and this is due to the solubility and mobility in the landfill site and migration of contaminants from the landfill site. It is seen that the sample in the location Mettukuppam Pillayar Koil street was also highly ambiguous. This shows the migration of the contaminants from the landfill site (Table 5.8.1, Figure 5.8.1).

▼ **Table 5.8.1:** Average Copper Content (mg/l) in Pre-monsoon and Post-monsoon Period

Location	Well Type	Pre-Monsoon	Post-Monsoon
Perungudi-Elumalai-house	PE	0.01	0.04
Perungudi-Thirumalainagar	PT	0.00	0.03
Thuraipakkam-shanmugam-house	TS	0.01	0.03
Thuraipakkam-Adiparasakthi k. m	TA	0.01	0.04
Thuraipakkam-Jayabalan-house	TJ	0.01	0.03
Mettukuppam Pillaiyar Koil street	MP	0.00	0.02
Perungudi-Elumalai-house	PE	0.01	0.02
Perungudi-Thirumalainagar	PT	0.00	0.03
Thuraipakkam-shanmugam-house	TS	0.01	0.02
Thuraipakkam-Adiparasakthi k. m	TA	0.01	0.02

Location	Well Type	Pre-Monsoon	Post-Monsoon
Thuraipakkam-Jayabalan-house	TJ	0.01	0.03
Mettukuppam Pillaiyar Koil street	MP	0.00	0.02

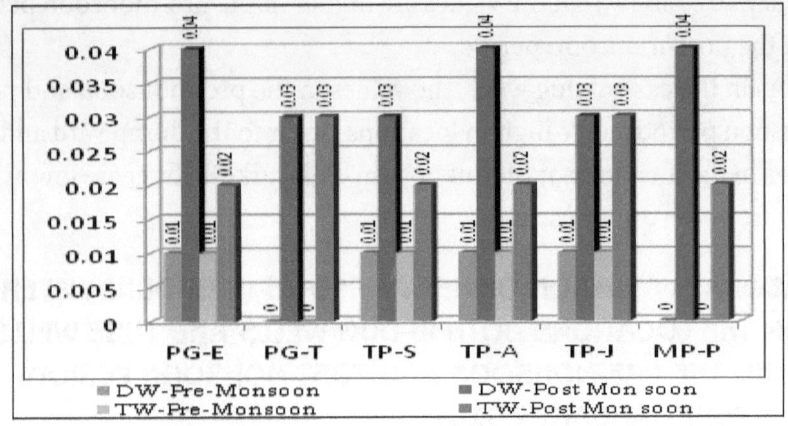

DW: DUG WELL; TW: TUBE WELL

▲ **Figure 5.8.1:** Average Copper Content (mg/i) in Pre-monsoon and Post-monsoon Period

Lead (mg/l)

From Figure 5.8.2, it is seen that the post-monsoon values are higher than the pre-monsoon values in all the cases. The values of the post-monsoon in dug wells are higher than the values of the pre-monsoon in tube wells in all the locations. This shows that the lead is migrating from the landfill site and the solubility of lead content in the landfill site is more for dug wells (Table 5.8.2, Figure 5.8.2)

Zinc (mg/l)

From Figure 5.8.3, it is seen that the post-monsoon values were higher than the pre-monsoon values in all the cases. In the location of Perungudi-Elumalai and Perungudi-Thirumalainagar, the post-monsoon and the pre-monsoon values are very high in tube wells when compared to dug wells. This shows that zinc is leached below, hence the values in tube wells when compared to dug wells. It has also been reported that a major portion of the total metal content in MSW is in inert form and is unlikely to go in a chemical reaction in landfills but will leach from the waste bed (Tessier et al, 1979) (Table 5.8.3, Figure 5.8.3).

Iron (mg/l)

From Figure 5.8.4, it is seen that the iron content during the pre-monsoon season was higher in the dug wells and tube wells than the post-monsoon period in all the locations. This effect is due to the dilution of metals in the post-monsoon period, hence the values are lower (Table 5.8.4, Figure 5.8.4).

Manganese (mg/l)

From Figure 5.8.5, it is inferred that the pre-monsoon values are higher in all locations when compared to post-monsoon values due to the dilution of metal in post-monsoon. The values in Thuraipakkam-Adiparasakthi location is high when compared to other location inferring that the manganese content may be very high; similarly, in Mettukuppam, Pillaiyarkoil street the values are low. This may be due to the distance from the dump yard. Thus the values in the locations differ due to the distance and depth from the dump yard both in the case of tube wells and dug wells (Table 5.8.5, Figure 5.8.5).

Nickel (mg/l)

From Figure 5.8.6, it is inferred that the pre-monsoon values in the dug wells are higher in almost all locations when compared to post-monsoon values due to dilution of metal in the post-monsoon. The values in Perungudi-Elumalai location for dug wells are very high as it is very close to the dump yard and the value is 0.08mg/l. Similarly, in tube wells, the value was very high in the location Thuraipakkam-Jayabalan (0.08mg/l) when compared to other locations, inferring that there may be variation in the nickel content from one location to other. Similarly, in Mettukuppam, Pillaiyarkoil street the values are low (0.01 to 0.03 mg/l). This may be due to the distance away from the landfill site (Table 5.8.6, Figure 5.8.6).

▼ **Table 5.8.2:** Average Lead Content (mg/l) in Pre-monsoon and Post-monsoon Period

Location	Well Type	Pre-Monsoon	Post-Monsoon
Perungudi-Elumalai-house	PE	0.05	0.06
Perungudi-Thirumalainagar	PT	0.02	0.06
Thuraipakkam-shanmugam-house	TS	0.05	0.08
Thuraipakkam-Adiparasakthi k. m	TA	0.02	0.10
Thuraipakkam-Jayabalan-house	TJ	0.07	0.05
Mettukuppam Pillaiyar Koil street	MP	0.06	0.04
Perungudi-Elumalai-house	PE	0.04	0.09
Perungudi-Thirumalainagar	PT	0.02	0.09
Thuraipakkam-shanmugam-house	TS	0.03	0.08
Thuraipakkam-Adiparasakthi k. m	TA	0.02	0.11
Thuraipakkam-Jayabalan-house	TJ	0.04	0.15
Mettukuppam Pillaiyar Koil street	MP	0.03	0.05

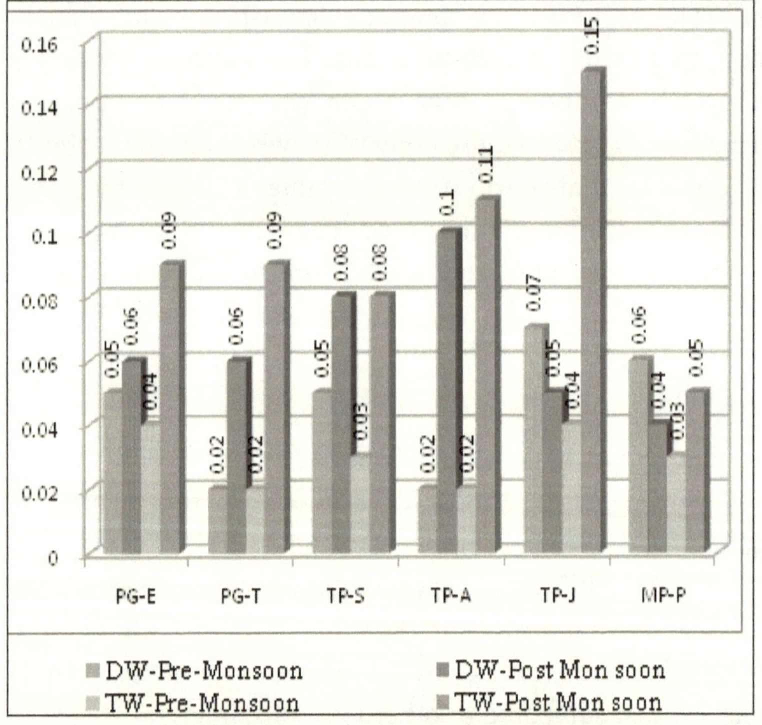

DW: DUG WELL; TW: TUBE WELL

▲ **Figure 5.8.2:** Average Lead Content (mg/i) in Pre-monsoon and Post-monsoon Period

▼ **Table 5.8.3:** Average Zinc Content (mg/l) in Pre-monsoon and Post-monsoon Period

Location	Well Type	Pre-Monsoon	Post-Monsoon
Perungudi-Elumalai-house	PE	0.03	0.06
Perungudi-Thirumalainagar	PT	0.05	0.08
Thuraipakkam-shanmugam-house	TS	0.03	0.03
Thuraipakkam-Adiparasakthi k. m	TA	0.10	0.31
Thuraipakkam-Jayabalan-house	TJ	0.03	0.09
Mettukuppam Pillaiyar Koil street	MP	0.10	0.25
Perungudi-Elumalai-house	PE	0.12	0.30
Perungudi-Thirumalainagar	PT	0.28	0.49
Thuraipakkam-shanmugam-house	TS	0.05	0.08
Thuraipakkam-Adiparasakthi k. m	TA	0.06	0.09
Thuraipakkam-Jayabalan-house	TJ	0.07	0.12
Mettukuppam Pillaiyar Koil street	MP	0.07	0.09

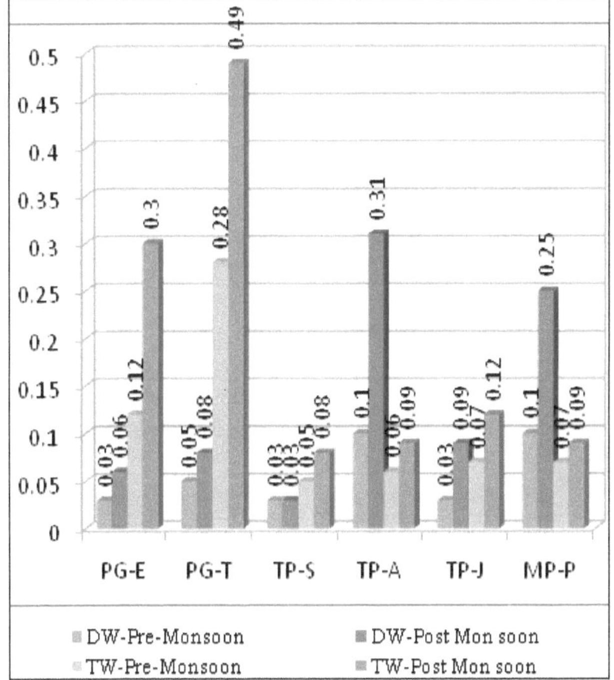

DW: DUG WELL; TW: TUBE WELL

▲ **Figure 5.8.3:** Average Zinc Content (mg/i) in Pre-monsoon and Post-monsoon Period

▼ **Table 5.8.4:** Average Iron Content (mg/l) in Pre-monsoon and Post-monsoon Period

Location	Well Type	Pre-Monsoon	Post-Monsoon
Perungudi-Elumalai-house	PE	0.16	0.12
Perungudi-Thirumalainagar	PT	0.16	0.13
Thuraipakkam-shanmugam-house	TS	0.12	0.04
Thuraipakkam-Adiparasakthi k. m	TA	0.11	0.07
Thuraipakkam-Jayabalan-house	TJ	0.07	0.05
Mettukuppam Pillaiyar Koil street	MP	0.08	0.06
Perungudi-Elumalai-house	PE	0.06	0.04
Perungudi-Thirumalainagar	PT	0.10	0.05
Thuraipakkam-shanmugam-house	TS	0.05	0.03
Thuraipakkam-Adiparasakthi k. m	TA	0.19	0.06
Thuraipakkam-Jayabalan-house	TJ	0.10	0.07
Mettukuppam Pillaiyar Koil street	MP	0.12	0.06

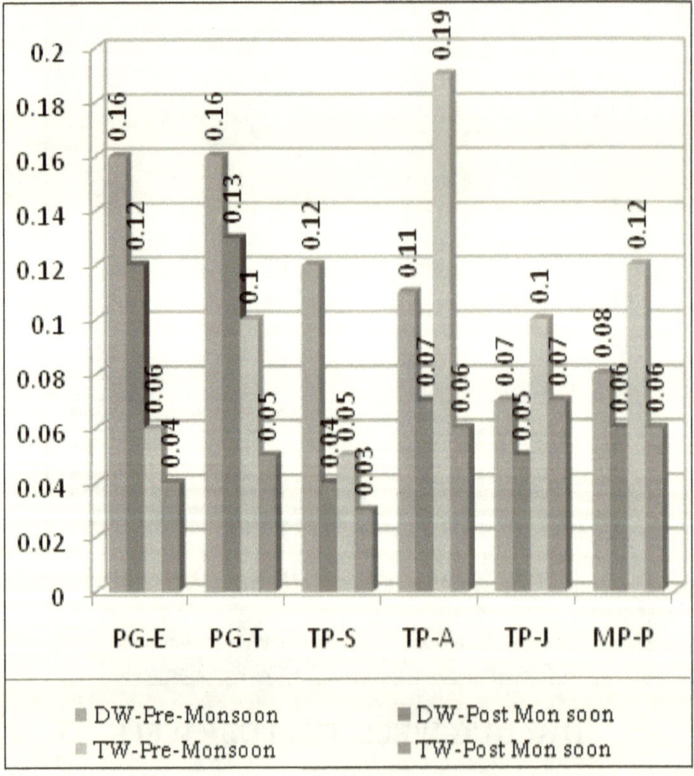

DW: DUG WELL; TW: TUBE WELL

▲ **Figure 5.8.4:** Average Iron Content (mg/l) in Pre-monsoon and Post-monsoon Period

▼ **Table 5.8.5:** Average Manganese Content (mg/l) in Pre-monsoon and Post-monsoon Period

Location	Well Type	Pre-Monsoon	Post-Monsoon
Perungudi-Elumalai-house	PE	0.44	0.23
Perungudi-Thirumalainagar	PT	0.50	0.09
Thuraipakkam-shanmugam-house	TS	0.34	0.02
Thuraipakkam-Adiparasakthi k. m	TA	0.98	0.80
Thuraipakkam-Jayabalan-house	TJ	0.04	0.00
Mettukuppam Pillaiyar Koil street	MP	0.15	0.04
Perungudi-Elumalai-house	PE	0.72	0.09
Perungudi-Thirumalainagar	PT	0.68	0.05
Thuraipakkam-shanmugam-house	TS	0.09	0.05
Thuraipakkam-Adiparasakthi k. m	TA	0.66	0.06
Thuraipakkam-Jayabalan-house	TJ	0.09	0.01
Mettukuppam Pillaiyar Koil street	MP	0.23	0.15

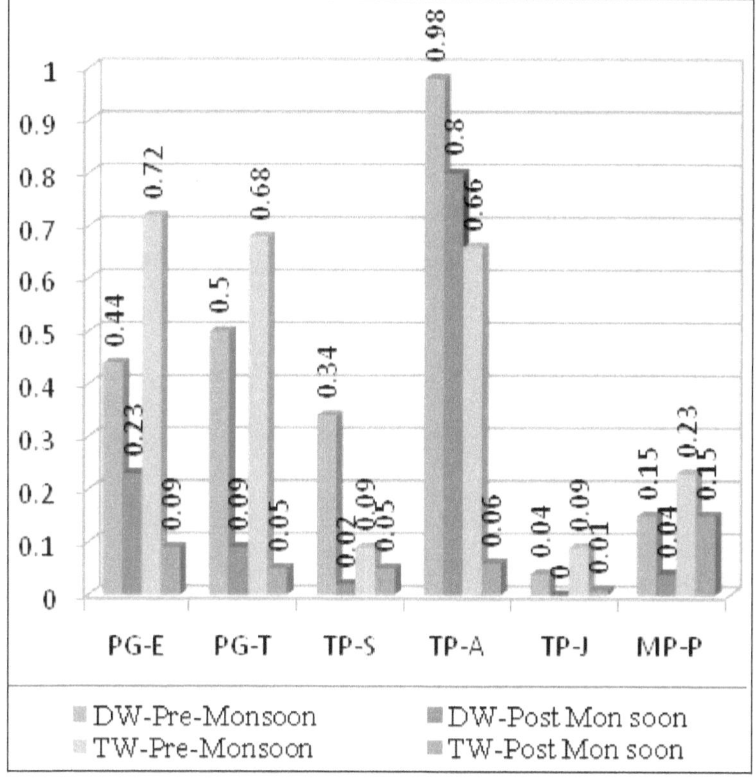

DW: DUG WELL; TW: TUBE WELL

▲ **Figure 5.8.5:** Average Manganese Content (mg/i) in Pre-monsoon and Post-monsoon Period

▼ **Table 5.8.6:** Average Nickel Content (mg/l) in Pre-monsoon and Post-monsoon Period

Location	Well Type	Pre-Monsoon	Post-Monsoon
Perungudi-Elumalai-house	PE	0.08	0.01
Perungudi-Thirumalainagar	PT	0.03	0.02
Thuraipakkam-shanmugam-house	TS	0.01	0.01
Thuraipakkam-Adiparasakthi k. m	TA	0.02	0.00
Thuraipakkam-Jayabalan-house	TJ	0.00	0.02
Mettukuppam Pillaiyar Koil street	MP	0.03	0.01
Perungudi-Elumalai-house	PE	0.03	0.00
Perungudi-Thirumalainagar	PT	0.03	0.01
Thuraipakkam-shanmugam-house	TS	0.01	0.01
Thuraipakkam-Adiparasakthi k. m	TA	0.02	0.38
Thuraipakkam-Jayabalan-house	TJ	0.08	0.00
Mettukuppam Pillaiyar Koil street	MP	0.02	0.01

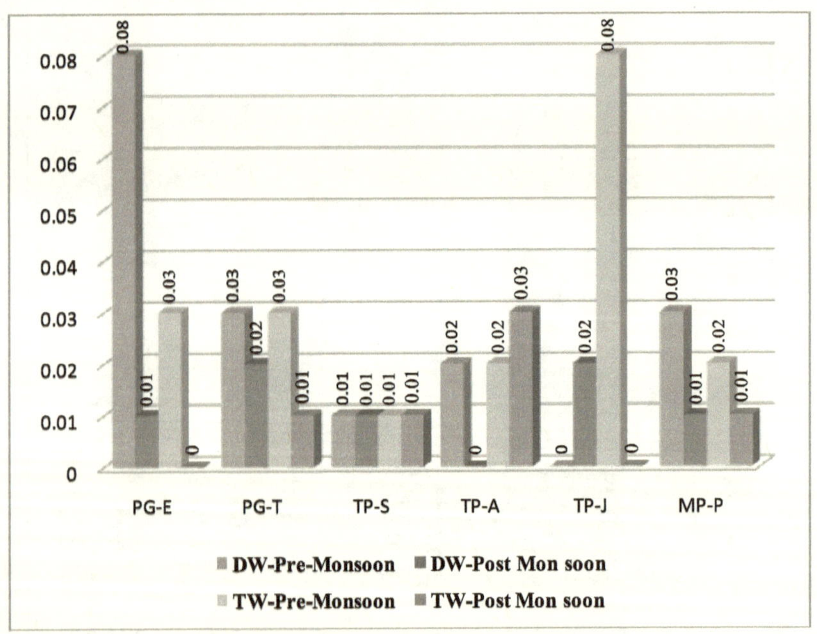

DW: DUG WELL; TW: TUBE WELL

▲ **Figure 5.8.6:** Average Nickel Content (mg/l) in the Pre-monsoon and Post-monsoon Period

EFFECT OF DEPTH OF THE WELLS AND DISTANCE OF THE LOCATION FROM THE PERUNGUDI DUMP YARD

The vertical extent of contamination of groundwater quality due to landfill waste depends on the distance, depth, and level of connectivity within the same aquifers, between the aquifers, and in the case of multiple aquifers. The dug wells here have a depth between 15 meters and tube wells have a depth of 40-45 meters. As it is seen in the case of copper, iron, and manganese, the values are very higher in the dug wells than tube wells in the same locations for pre-monsoon and post-monsoon. This is due to the interference of the landfill at the places affected by the contamination, a shallow aquifer showing higher concentration. The locations selected are 2 km from the Perungudi dumpyard. In the above study, it is seen that the locations near the landfill areas have high values and are found to decrease with increasing distance from landfill sites as in the case of Mettukuppam Pillayar Koil street where it is away from landfill areas and the values are low.

FINDINGS

On analyzing the values of the various physico-chemical parameters for the different seasons in thirteen dug wells, nine tube wells, and four surface water samples, it is seen that the pH is alkaline in nature in all the water samples. The EC content in the post-monsoon period reduces due to the rains which dilute the water. In the present study, the TDS in all the water samples were high and exceeded the desired limit of the CPHEEO, (1999). In the case of total hardness, the values are higher during the pre-monsoon period and exceed the maximum allowable limit. Calcium, magnesium, potassium, sulfate, bicarbonate values are higher in the pre-monsoon period than in the post-monsoon periods due to dilution that takes place during rains. The nitrate content is higher in the pre-monsoon periods and in chloride, fluoride, and nitrate the values in the water samples exceed the desirable level by CPHEEO, 1999.

Both in the case of COD and BOD, the values in the water samples are higher in pre-monsoon and lower in the post-monsoon period.

In the case of heavy metals, the average lead content in the water samples is above the desirable limits of CPHEEO (1999) both in the pre- and post-monsoon periods. A similar pattern was seen in copper, nickel, iron, and manganese. The water sample values are below the desirable limit of CPHEEO (1999) in the case of zinc. Cadmium and chromium content in the water samples are within the desirable values of CPHEEO, (1999), and only in locations close to the dump yard, the levels were above the desirable level.

The suburbs of Chennai are expanding rapidly with a huge increase in the influx of population. Long spells of water shortages combined with rapid and haphazard urbanization have led to the overexploitation of the precious water bodies. Mindless dumping of sewage and garbage into the freshwater lakes has affected them seriously.

The chemical properties such as chloride, sulfate, and pH are analyzed and the results in the year 2002 are compared with the results of the same site being carried out in the year 1999. From the comparative results, it is noticed that within three years of span there is a two to three-fold increase in the contamination levels of soil and water. It is also noticed that there is a reduced concentration level of contamination in soil and water as the radial distance increase from the dumping source in the Pallikaranai Marsh (Padmavathi, 2008).

Vasanthi et al, (2008) discuss the chemical analyses that were carried out on water samples collected at various radial distances from the boundary of the dumping yard at intervals of 3 months and for a period of three years. The study has revealed that the groundwater quality does not conform to the drinking water quality standards as per the Bureau of Indian Standards.

Similarly, in the present study, it revealed the above-mentioned finding where within the radial distance of 2 km, the water quality does not confirm the desirable water quality standards as per CPHEEO (1999).

The outcome of the analysis of water samples of the Study area reveals that the pH is alkaline, which reduces the solubility of metals. Most of the physico-chemical values of the water samples exceed the desirable level of CPHEEO (1999). Excess total hardness in the water when consumed causes urinary concretions and diseases of the kidney or bladder; a high concentration of magnesium causes laxative effects. High levels of sodium are harmful to persons suffering from cardiac, renal, and circulatory diseases and a high concentration of chloride is considered as an indicator of pollution. Most of the heavy metals exceed the desirable level of CPHEEO (1999) and lead to toxic effects or bio-magnification in the aquatic environment.

SOCIO-ECONOMIC CHARACTERISTICS OF THE POPULATION AND THEIR WILLINGNESS TO PAY FOR CONSERVATION AND MANAGEMENT OF THE PALLIKARANAI WETLAND

INTRODUCTION

Wetlands provide many important services to human society but are at the same time ecologically sensitive systems. The valuation of wetlands' ecological services is a relatively recent phenomenon. Historically, wetlands were viewed as a waste of valuable land that could only be 'improved' through drainage and destruction of the wetland. Today, while there is now widespread recognition that wetlands provide valuable ecological services, there remains substantial debate over whether particular areas are in their highest economic use as wetlands, and to what extent public and private resources should be used for their protection and restoration. Hence, there is a growing need to quantify the value of wetland services (Mitsch and Gosselink, 2000).

The services provided by wetlands include habitat for species, protection against floods, water purification, amenities, and recreational opportunities. Because these services typically have no market price, a measure of their values can only be obtained through non-market valuation techniques. Many wetland valuation studies have been conducted and the range of the estimates is remarkable.

The urban wetlands extend numerous economic, environmental, and social benefits in terms of recharging groundwater table, maintenance of soil moisture, microclimatic effects like temperature, and moisture control, control of floods, maintenance of flora-fauna relationship and maintenance of biodiversity, provide recreation to local people and the visitors and offer educational aspect. Urban wetlands have been utilized as natural cleansing agents to mitigate the additional pollutant levels introduced within the urban landscape. They absorb large amounts of point source pollutants like sewage, solid waste, industrial waste, and from the washing of vehicles and those which 'runaway' from their source like agricultural fields, hospitals, open garbage dumps in rainwater. The typical run-off from cities carries iron, lead, copper, as well as the other heavy metals, toxins, phosphorous, nitrogen, and hydrocarbons, acids.

Wetlands can be found in many urban areas in India and such urban wetlands have been the lifeline of most cities in India. Cities of Bhopal, Bangalore, Chennai, Udaipur, Hyderabad, Indore, Sagar, Raipur are a few examples to quote. Once upon a time, these urban wetlands maintained a steady supply of water for the city, recharged the groundwater, cooled the city, and prevented floods as they were a natural drainage system. Over the years, these very tanks and wetlands have been neglected, encroached upon either to accommodate more houses or to dump waste. This has caused large-scale water crisis and monsoon flooding and waterlogging, leading to misery, and diseases. Thus, the very existence of the wetlands is in danger. These wetlands have often been used as open access resources as an easily accessible source of various resources and 'wastelands' as the most convenient and costless dumpsites. Various uses have been extracted without making any investment for the maintenance and restoration of these wetlands (Verma, 2001).

Having discussed on the extent of degradation and threats, reduction in the area of wetland with time-changes in land use /land cover area of wetland with time, water quality deterioration in wetlands due to anthropogenic activities mainly the municipal solid dumping and letting out sewerage in wetlands, the wetland valuation is very much required to be undertaken so as to cover the extent of monetary benefit or loss to various stakeholders in case benefits are directly or indirectly marketed or people's perception for the conservation of wetland resource was sought in the absence of any such markets.

The lack of pricing of wetland functions as well as the lack of cost recovery mechanisms have been the key determinants of inefficient and often inappropriate and excessive use of wetlands (Turner et. al, 2003). In this regard, it has been cited that a significant step in determining what should be done about environmental damage is to value it (in economic terms) and compare it with the cost of preventing the damage (World Bank, 1992). Biodiversity valuation particularly in developing countries like India assumes added importance to justify/supplement the conservation measures in the existing development-environment trade-off scenario. In the absence of market prices for environmental resources, economists have devised various techniques to estimate the economic value of non-marketable resources (Freeman, 1993). The dominant measure of economic value has been the WTP for a specific improvement in an environmental resource or service (Binilkumar and Ramanathan, 2009).

In the economic valuation methods, the contingent valuation method (CVM) uses surveys of expressed preferences to evaluate WTP for (generally) non-market, environmental goods. This approach gives the method, in theory, wide applicability to an extensive range of use and passive-use values associated with such goods. Only one known valuation approach, CVM, can in principle provide useful information about the economic significance of lost passive-use values when ecosystems are degraded or destroyed by pollution and/or development. CVM is based on the direct elicitation of passive-use (and other use) values from individuals through the use of sample surveys (administered via direct interview or mail or telephone-based questionnaires). Typically, CVM provides respondents with information about hypothetical (and occasionally real) environmental loss situations and then goes on to ask respondents for their WTP to prevent such losses (Bateman, 1993).

The open-ended approach in the CVM is convenient to answer, does not require an interviewer, and does not result in any starting point bias. For those studies which aim at deriving a value that would provide a conservative estimate, the open-ended approach would be efficient in the sense that this approach would provide a lower level conservative value than the bidding game approach (Walsh et al, 1984).

The application of CVM to measure the WTP for the conservation and management of the Pallikaranai Marsh to obtain the WTP. In the CVM questionnaire, the main formats of the core valuation questions in the open-ended (OE) method.

METHODOLOGY-DESIGNING A SURVEY TO OBTAIN INFORMATION ON THE PERCEPTION AND WTP IN THE ENVIRONMENTAL STUDIES

Chennai is the capital city of Tamil Nadu with a 7.8% growth rate in population during the last 10 years (2001-11). A large part of South Chennai was historically a flood place as evidenced by the soil type of the region. The numerous smaller wetlands that surrounded the Pallikaranai Marsh served as the only source of irrigation for that area, which thrived on paddy cultivation. This gave the marsh a legendary status since the villages did not have wells or dug out ponds, which are the norm in the northern districts of Tamil Nadu (Vencatesan, 2007).

Although the entire South Chennai is affected by the environmental degradation and dumping of garbage in the Pallikaranai Marshland, it is not possible to collect data from all localities due to the time and cost constraints of an individual researcher. Moreover, there is no household-level survey data available from secondary sources to study the socio-economic conditions of the population in and around Pallikaranai Marsh. Hence, it has been decided to confirm the study area within one kilometer in and around of Pallikaranai Marsh area. People residing in these localities are more affected due to environmental degradation than areas away from the Marsh There are several residential localities, consisting of one to two streets, called with a different prefix of Nagar. There are localities within the radius of one kilometer and five localities are selected residential localities (in local government it is called wards) as a simple random sample method.

The selected wards are presented below.
1. Balaji Nagar
2. Kamakshi Nagar
3. Rajesh Nagar
4. Ma. Po. Si. Nagar
5. Quaid Millaith Nagar

A list of households in each of these localities was prepared. A random sample of 20% of households was selected at random using a simple random sampling method.

Before the main survey, the pre-testing of the interview schedule was undertaken in the area. The draft interview schedule was prepared prior to pre-testing, which consisted of three major parts discussed in the following section.

The Questionnaire contains the following components:

The first part of the questionnaire aims at recording the information about the respondent and his or her family members, attitudes toward the wetland, and particularly their belief in the feasibility of wetland conservation. Along with these questions, respondents are presented with a list of environmental characteristics and activities and are asked to indicate the ones related to the wetland.

In the second part, an introductory text explains the purpose of the survey and presents the scenario for the conservation and management of Pallikaranai Wetland. At the time of the survey, locals were already aware of the planned interventions (explanation of these interventions somewhere else in the thesis is important), so it is reasonable to assume that respondents would consider the scenario adequately realistic. The presentation of the scenario is quite detailed since it deals with the contingent valuation part.

The third part of the questionnaire was the socio-economic details of the respondent and their households.

Before conducting the final survey the questionnaire was subjected to two rounds of 'pre-testing' (Arrow et al, 1993). The respondents for pre-testing were selected from all areas of the study region to accommodate the site-specific factors influencing the behavior of the households (Venkatachalam, 2004). In this study, the first round of pre-testing was done in the month of November 2008 for a period of six days and the second round of pre-testing was done in the month of January 2009, for a period of 15 days. The inputs from the first round of pre-testing were used to improve the overall structure of the interview schedule. The purpose of the second round was to strengthen the contingent valuation scenarios as well as some of the other aspects of the remaining contingent valuation component. A copy of the questionnaire is given in Annexure III.

In order to control the interview bias, one of the important points highlighted in the NOAA panel report is that 'in-person interview' is desirable but at the same time steps have to be taken to reduce the interviewer bias as well (Arrow et al, 1993). Initially, the researcher experienced various problems with many of the households in the focus group, which were suspected to lead to 'non-response.' The reasons identified are the general tendency of the households not only in the town but also in many parts of Tamil Nadu to not reveal any information about their demographic and economic status to an 'outsider,' which they think would affect their food ration provided through the government-run fair price shops. More precisely, the poorer sections of the households who are entitled to purchasing goods from fair price shops at cheaper rates have the tendency to overstate the actual household size and understate the actual household income. In this case, the households became highly co-operative during pre-testing, because the households seemed to have realized that the researcher was an independent person who could be relied upon.

During the initial survey, the potential bias that we initially encountered in the field was the interviewer bias. When we initially went around the study area, the households treated us like an 'outsider.' Later we started speaking in the local language i. e., Tamil for which they felt comfortable. We had taken the help of the local self-help group ladies, who volunteered to come with us to interact with the respondent initially.

The interview schedule was designed in such a way that various responses can be cross-checked with multiple questions. Pre-testing the contingent valuation part in a rigorous manner helped the researcher to completely refine the scenarios described in the initial version. The respondents were asked to answer all the questions in the interview schedule and were asked to state their own preferences on all aspects in an open-ended way.

In a Contingent Valuation (CV) study, a description of the commodity to be valued is an essential part (Mitchell and Carson, 1989). In the present study, commodity valued is the conservation of the wetland for quality drinking water. The respondent may consider the conservation of the Pallikaranai Marsh in order to get quality drinking water in the future.

The Researcher has discussed with the stakeholders regarding the quality drinking water and also led them to the perception of the environmental problems in Chennai and the study area in particular. The researcher also could address the major environmental problems in and around the Pallikaranai Marsh which has polluted the water in the wetland.

In this study, all the respondents were aware of the environmental problems in the marsh, they were willing to save the marsh and hence no protest bid is seen.

The nature of the 'payment vehicle' used in CV scenarios itself is another source that may potentially attract bias and hence, the payment vehicle used in the CV scenarios should be neutral and bias-free (Arrow et al, 1993, Mitchell and Carson, 1989). Most CV studies generally use customized payment vehicles which are determined during the process of pre-testing (Portney, 1994). This being the case, we decided to use a payment vehicle that is acceptable by all and which would be free from biases. The proposed conservation program is a hypothetical 'Pallikaranai Wetland Conservation Fund' to which households can contribute money for the preservation and management of wetlands. The payment vehicle here was an 'Annual fee' for conserving the Pallikaranai Marsh for quality drinking water and the respondents were informed that they would pay the amount every year.

The choice of elicitation format employed in the present study was based on the respondent, as they were asked to state their WTP for the conservation of wetland through an 'open-ended' format. In the present study, the respondents discussed with their families and stated the WTP.

One of the problems that we encountered during the construction of the final CV scenario was that for the conservation of the marsh, how this could be quantified. During the pre-testing rounds, the respondent felt that the need for conservation of the marsh by stopping garbage dumping in the marsh, sewerage water to enter the marsh, encroachment, etc. To get quality drinking water in the future, the respondents valued the perceptions mentioned above.

Till now, we discussed the administrative and methodological procedures we followed while conducting the CV survey in our study area so that we could obtain the 'valid' CV results. We discussed various steps and precautions taken to eliminate some of the biases at the survey stage itself. As the CV studies for valuing quality drinking water by conserving the marsh especially in developing countries are limited, the present study followed various standard guidelines and measures available from the broader CV literature to ensure that the results derived in a developing country context could be used for useful policy-making purposes; moreover, by using scientific methods we ensured that our study could play a good model for future CV studies especially, in the area of economic valuation of wetlands.

SURVEY DESIGN, SAMPLING METHOD, QUESTIONNAIRE, AND DATA COLLECTION.

The CV survey for the valuation of wetland functions was conducted using a carefully designed questionnaire, following the NOAA panel's guidelines. The final version of the questionnaire was formulated after a pilot survey with open-ended WTP questions. The questionnaire consists of three parts (Mitchell and Carson, 1989) of which the first asks general questions, the second presents WTP questions and the third includes respondents' socio-economic characteristics.

The household interview was conducted among the adult members of the sample households who were above 18 years old. In some of the households, it was observed that both men and women tried to answer the questions simultaneously. However, only one member was requested to answer all the questions in the interview schedule but consultation with the other household members was allowed. In some of the sample households where the men were absent during the interview, the women desired to discuss with the men before answering some of the questions such as household income, WTP value, etc., these respondents were approached subsequently to obtain answers for these questions.

Initially, the researcher introduced herself self to people and the purpose of my visit/study to the people. They realized the need for such a study and they acknowledged me. So the questionnaire was filled with the information's given by the respondents. Giving the respondents enough time and the briefing of questions made me comfortable and useful to me. Briefed in Tamil and questions were asked in the native language. The final survey was conducted from July to September 2009.

SOCIO-ECONOMIC CHARACTERISTICS AND PERCEPTION OF RESPONDENTS ON ENVIRONMENTAL ISSUES OF PALLIKARANAI MARSH.

The questionnaire was described by me in such a way, covering all the issues like their general living conditions, sources of income, and environment-related problems. Since the study was aimed at conservation and management of the marsh for acquiring quality drinking water. By this, the WTP of the community to protect the marsh can be listed.

Socio-Economic Characteristics of Respondents

In the following paragraphs, we discuss the socio-economic characteristics of respondents in Tables 6.4.1.1 to 6.4.1.6.

Out of the total respondents of 233, 166 (71%) respondents are women and 67 (29%) respondents are men (Figure 6.4.1.1). There were more women who were ready to come forward as they felt the need to get quality drinking water. All the respondents belong to the age group above 18 years and below 70 years (Figure 6.4.1.2). Most of the respondents are middle-aged, who have the ability to provide various information as well as make decisions on behalf of the households. While more than 40% of the men reported that they were born in this area and more than 60% of the women said that they came to town only after their marriage. Even though they were uneducated or with no occupation, they felt the need to save the marsh especially from the sewerage water let in the marsh and the garbage dumping taking place in the marsh area.

The Figure 6.4.1.3 shows that, out of the 233 households, nearly 66% (153) of the households are found to be living in this area for less than 25 years, 23% (54) of households are found to be living in this area for about 25-50 years and 11% (26) households are living here for >50 years.

The family size of the households of the respondents ranges from 1 to 14 numbers. Out of the 233 households, 78 (33%) of households live in a family of four and 59 (25%) of households live in a family of five. This implies that the sample households are typical urban family. Nineteen households only live in a family size of more than seven members. Three respondents have a family size of 9, 11, and 14 (Figure 6.4.1.4).

A look at Figure 6.4.1.5 on the educational qualification of the respondents reveals that the 56 (24%) respondents are uneducated and have not received any formal education. 106 (45%) respondents have studied between 6-10th standard. There are only four professionals out of the total number of respondents. It is also seen that 20 (9%) respondents have studied >10th standard.

In the present study, the income of the respondents both women and men have been taken into consideration. The income range of the men and women respondents shows that 42 of the respondents who are women have no income. 139 respondents have an income range of up to Rs. 3500/. Out of 139 respondents, 105 are women, and 34 are men. 42 respondents have an income between Rs. 3500 to 7,500. Of which, 23 are men, and 19 are women. It is seen that the income earned by the ten men respondent is >Rs. 7500/-. But the women respondents did not get such high income when compared to men. Most of the men and women respondents have a low income which is up to Rs. 3500/. The respondents chosen in this study are generally from a poorer background (Figure 6.4.1.6).

All the tables related to the Annexure IV (Tables 6.4.1.7 to 6.4.1.12) are discussed below. It is seen that the men respondents are engaged in some occupations. There are only 8 (12%) of the men respondents who are into government jobs and the rest 40 (60%) of the men respondents are self-employed. They are self-employed as are into carpentry, masonry, shopkeepers, etc. 42 women respondent out of 166 are without any occupation. They prefer to stay at home in order to take care of the children and elders and some of them due to health problems stay at home. The study reveals that 100 (61%) respondents who are women are self-employed. They work in petty shops, own small shops, or do some petty works, household work in other nearby flats. 20 (12%) of the respondents work in private companies nearby area. It is seen that 121 (52%) respondents have only one member in their households who are employed, 95 respondents (41%) have only two members employed in their households. Similarly, 11 respondents (5%) show three employed and six respondent (2%) shows four employed in their respective households. Regarding the source of water in the households for the respondents, most of them use the public tap. Only 16 respondents have individual connections, two respondents have hand pumps, and two respondents have their own well. Two of the respondents informed that there was no water source near their area. It is seen that 120 (51%) of the respondents have both radio and television. All the respondents were exposed to the means of dissemination of news and other topics where the respondent are aware of what is happening around them and all over the world. It was also seen that 200 (86%) respondents use both cookers and fans in their houses as they are minimum basic needs for themselves. 134 (57%) respondents use motorcycles and nearly 86 (37%) respondents do not own a vehicle.

Having discussed the important socio-economic characteristics of the households, let us move on to the perception of respondents on environmental issues of Pallikaranai Marsh discussed below.

Perception of Respondents on Environmental Issues of Pallikaranai Marsh

In the following paragraphs, we discuss the perception of the respondents on the environmental issues of Pallikaranai Marsh in Tables 6.4.2.1 to 6.4.2.6.

The opinion of the respondents on the various major problems faced in Chennai and in the Pallikaranai Marsh is shown in Figure 6.4.2.1. It is seen that environmental problems including quality drinking water are the major and very important problem. Nearly 150 respondents out of 233 opine that this problem was very important. Similarly, as per the opinion of the respondents, education followed by crime than corruption and lastly unemployment were in the order of importance.

The respondents also shared their opinion on the most important problem in and around the Pallikaranai Marsh. It was seen that the solid waste dumping was the most important problem as out of 233 respondents, 170 opine that it was the most important problem. This was followed by sewerage, increasing population, and lastly encroachment (Figure 6.4.2.2).

Figure 6.4.2.3 shows that the respondents expressed that the water quality of the marsh has totally deteriorated and is unfit for consumption. Out of 233 respondents, 150 (64%) respondents expressed that the water quality of the marsh should be improved. Nearly 40 (18%) respondents have expressed that garbage dumping should be stopped in the marsh to prevent water and air pollution in and around the marsh. Similarly, 36 respondents (15%) expressed that sewerage water should not be allowed in the marsh area. Lastly, 7 respondents (3%) opine that encroachment in the marshland is very critical due to which the area of the marsh is shrinking.

From the Figure 6.4.2.4, it is seen that the nearly 150 respondents opine that the drinking water is the most important service which they could receive from the Pallikaranai Marsh followed by recreation and tourism (29%), employment to fishermen (4%), and stability of microclimate (2%)

As we have discussed in the previous chapters that Pallikaranai Marsh is being affected by the entry of sewerage water and garbage dumped in the marsh, encroachments, etc. In the present survey, it was seen that 206 (88.5%) respondents are of the opinion that the marsh is highly polluted, 15 (6.5%) opine that the marsh is moderately polluted and 12 (5%) marginally polluted. (Figure 6.4.2.5). It is also seen that 222 (95%) respondents rate the water quality of the marsh as 'worst' and 11 (5%) opine that it is 'bad' (Figure 6.4.2.6).

▼ **Table 6.4.1.1:** Gender Distribution Among Respondents

Gender	Number of respondents	Percentage
Men	67	29
Women	166	71
TOTAL	233	100

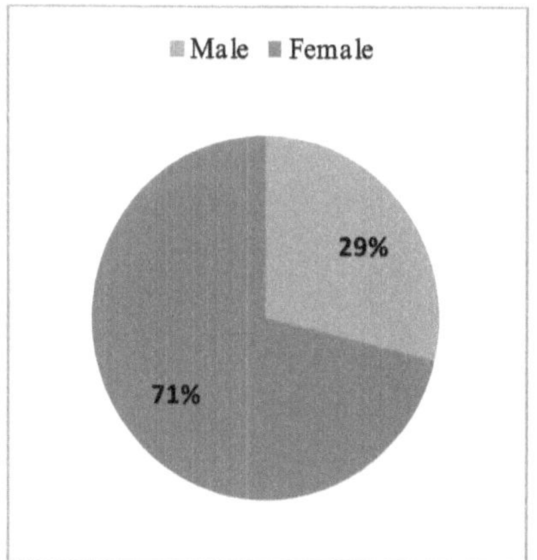

▲ **Figure 6.4.1.1:** Gender Distribution Among Respondents

▼ **Table 6.4.1.2:** Age Distribution Among Respondents

Age	Number of respondents	Percentage
18-25 years	39	17
26-50 years	149	64
>50 years	45	19
Grand total	**233**	**100.00**

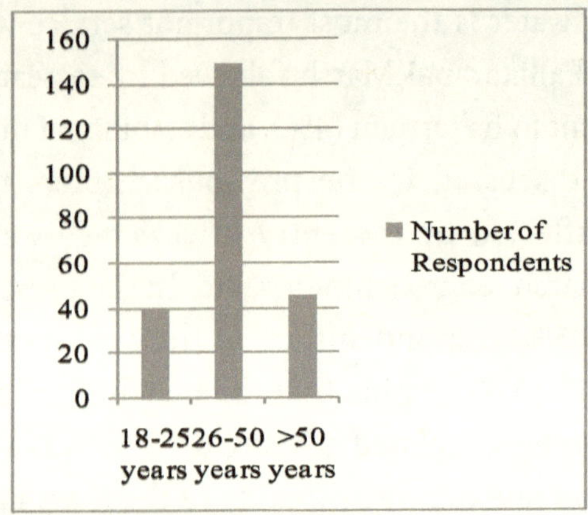

▲ **Figure 6.4.1.2:** Age Distribution Among Respondents

▼ **Table 6.4.1.3:** Number of Years Respondents Residing in the Pallikaranai Marsh Area

Number of years	Number of respondents	Percentage
1-25 years	153	66
25-50 years	54	23
>50 years	26	11
Grand total	**233**	**100**

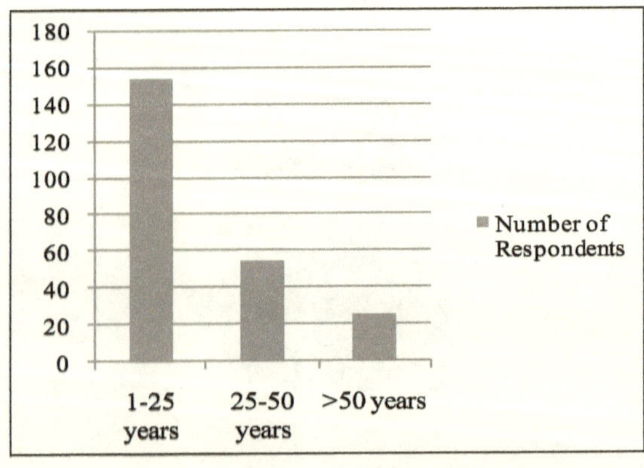

▲ **Figure 6.4.1.3:** Number of Years Residing in Pallikaranai Marsh Area

▼ **Table 6.4.1.4:** Family Size of the Respondents

Family size	Number of respondents	Percentage
1	6	3
2	22	9
3	29	12
4	78	33
5	59	25
6	20	9
7	11	5
8	5	2
9	1	0
11	1	0
14	1	0
Grand total	**233**	**100**

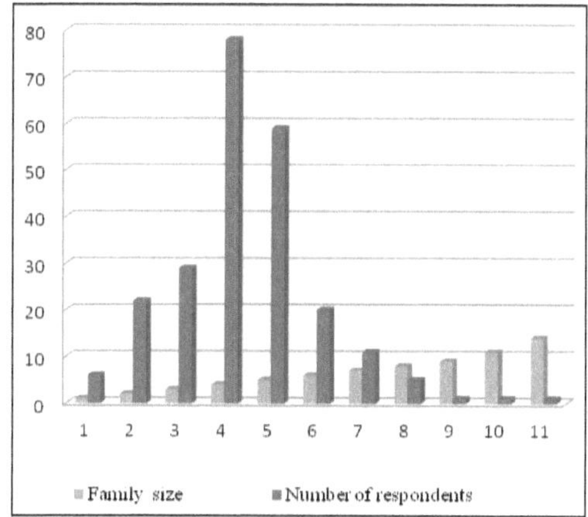

▲ **Figure 6.4.1.4:** Family Size of the Respondents

▼ **Table 6.4.1.5:** Educational Qualification of the Respondents

Educational qualification	Number of respondents	Percentage
Un educated	56	24
1-5th standard	47	20
6-10th standard	106	45
>10th standard	20	9
Professionals	4	2
Grand total	**233**	**100**

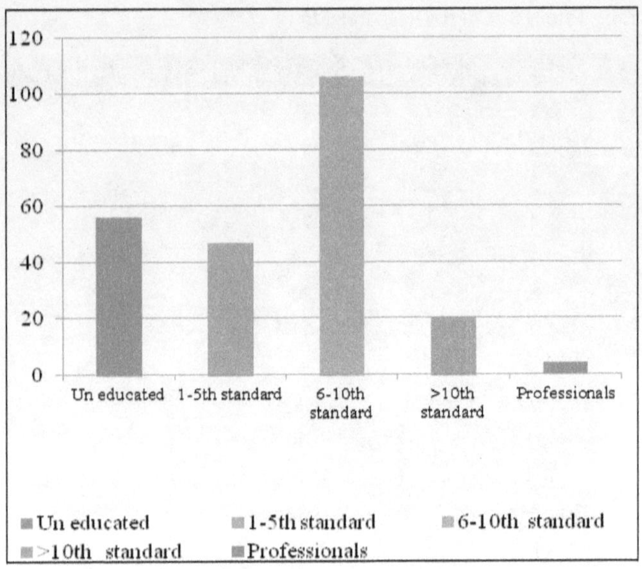

▲ **Figure 6.4.1.5:**   Educational Qualification of the Respondents

▼ **Table 6.4.1.6:**   Income Range of Men and Women Respondents

Income range	Men	Women	Total
No income	-	42	42
uptoRs. 3500	34	105	139
RS.3500 - 7500	23	19	42
>Rs. 7500	10	0	10
Grand total	**67**	**166**	**233**

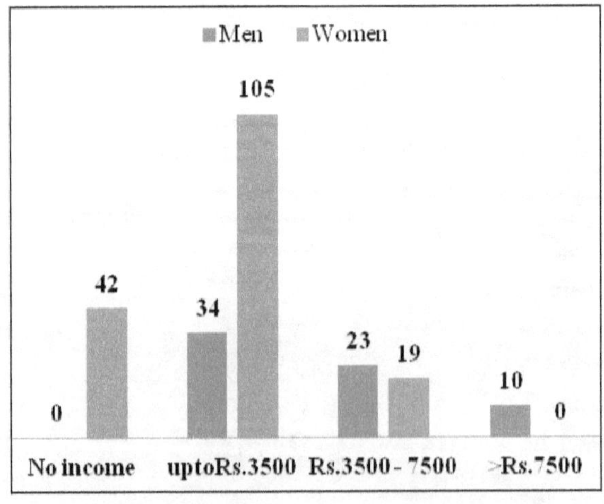

▲ **Figure 6.4.1.6:**   Income Range of Men and Women Respondents

PERCEPTION OF RESPONDENTS ON ENVIRONMENTAL ISSUES OF PALLIKARANAI MARSH

▼ **Table 6.4.2.1:** Opinion of the Respondents on the Various Major Problems Faced in Chennai

Opinion of the respondents	Unemployment	Crime	Education	Corruption	Environmental problems including water quality
Very important	4	70	150	146	155
Important	99	148	75	76	77
Not important	129	9	1	7	3
Don't know	1	6	2	4	3
Grand total	**233**	**233**	**233**	**233**	**233**

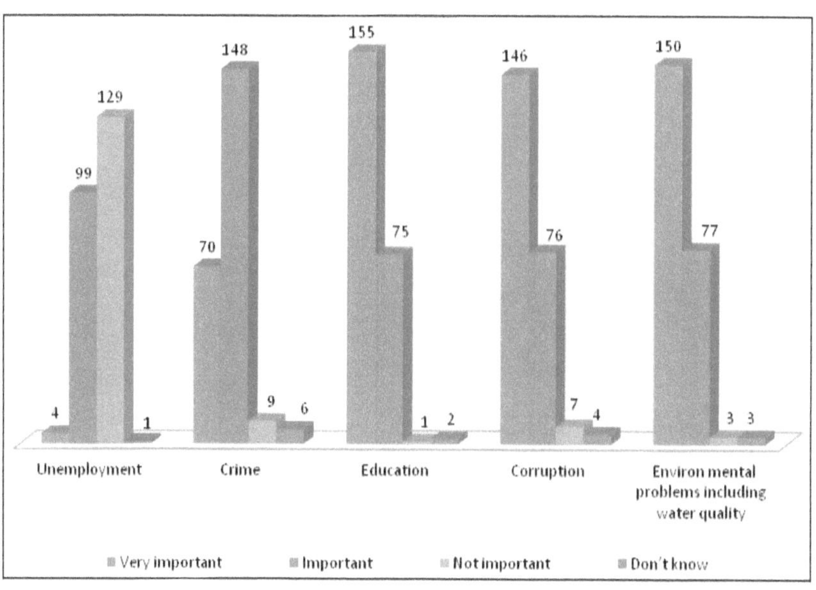

▲ **Figure 6.4.2.1:** Opinion of the Respondents on the Various Major Problems Faced in Chennai

▼ **Table 6.4.2.2:** Major Problems Which Are Ranked By the Respondents in and Around the Pallikaranai Marsh

Opinion of the respondents	Encroachment	Increasing population	Solid waste dumping	Sewerage
Most important problem	74	84	142	170
Very important problem	58	62	50	34
Important problem	51	49	29	27
Somewhat important problem	34	38	7	1
Least important problem	16	0	5	1
Grand total	**233**	**233**	**233**	**233**

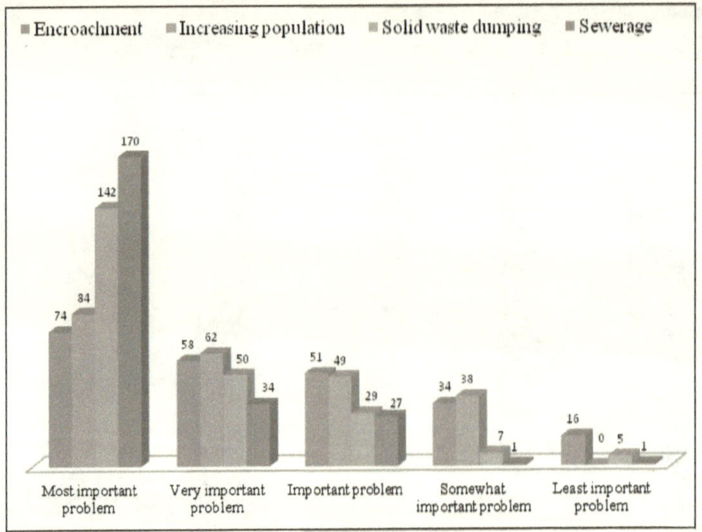

▲ **Figure 6.4.2.2:** Major Problems Which Are Ranked By the Respondents in and Around the Pallikaranai Marsh

▼ **Table 6.4.2.3:** Opinion of the Respondents as the Most Important Problem in the Pallikaranai Marsh

Problem	Respondents preference	Percentage
Encroachment	7	3
Water quality	150	64
Sewerage water	36	15
Garbage dumped	40	18
Grand total	**233**	**100**

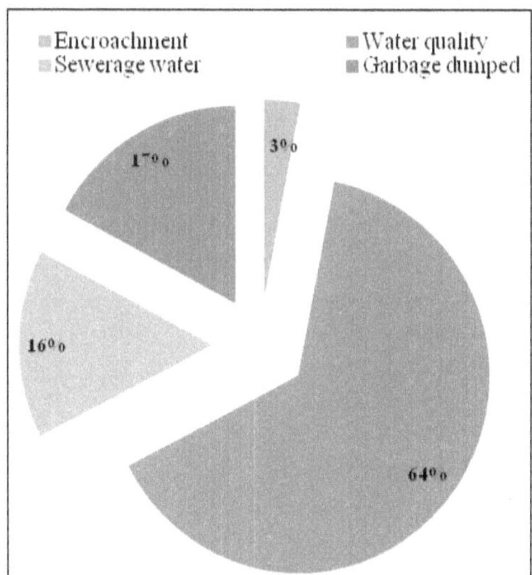

▲ **Figure 6.4.2.3:** Opinion of the Respondents as the Most Important Problem in the Pallikaranai Marsh

▼ **Table 6.4.2.4:** Service Ranking By the Respondents

Services ranking	Number of respondents	Percentage
Drinking water	150	65
Stability of microclimate	6	2
Employment to fishermen	10	4
Recreation and tourism	67	29
Total	**233**	**233**

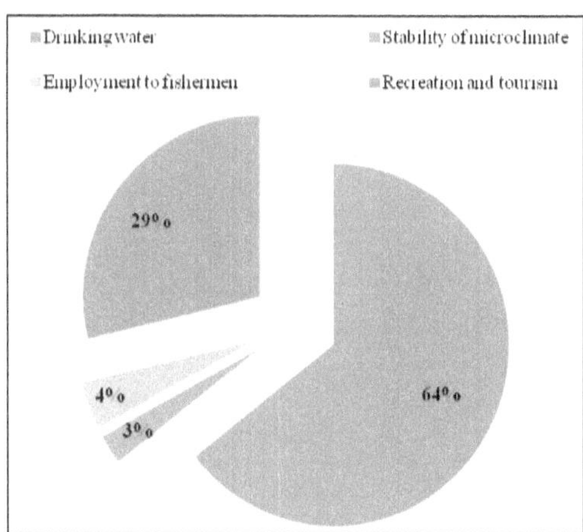

▲ **Figure 6.4.2.4:** Service Ranking of the Respondents

▼ **Table 6.4.2.5:** Respondents Opinion on Extent of Pollution in Pallikaranai Marsh

Extent of pollution	Number of respondents	Percentage
Marginally polluted	12	5
Moderately polluted	15	6.5
Highly polluted	206	88.5
TOTAL	233	100

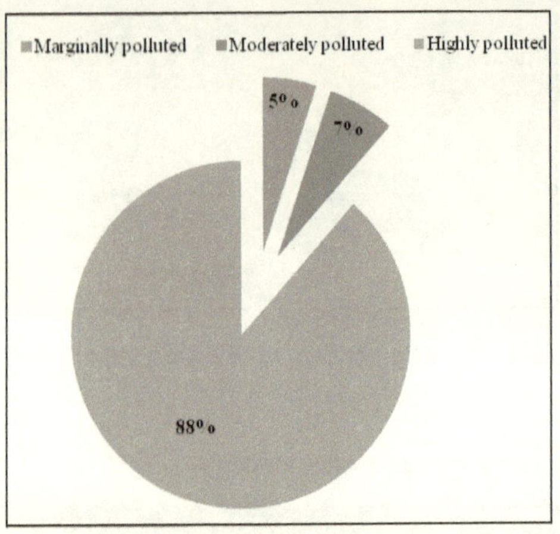

▲ **Figure 6.4.2.5:** Respondents Opinion on Extent of Pollution in Pallikaranai Marsh

▼ **Table 6.4.2.6:** Respondents Rating Pallikaranai Marsh with Respect to the Water Quality

Rating of Pallikaranai Marsh	Number of respondents	Percentage
WORST	222	95
BAD	11	5
TOTAL	233	100

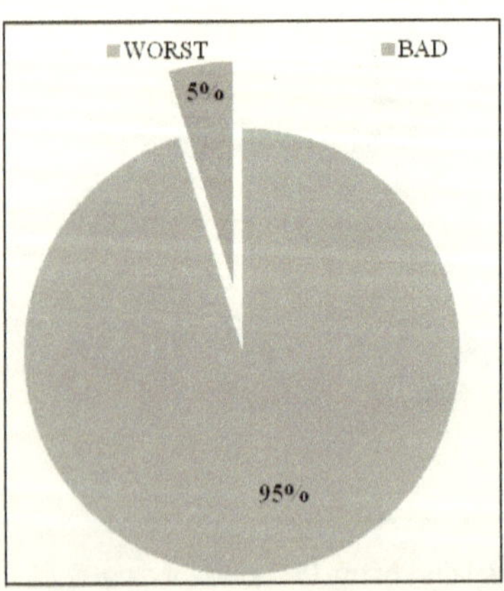

▲ **Figure 6.4.2.6:** Respondents Rating Pallikaranai Marsh with Respect to the Water Quality

WILLINGNESS TO PAY (WTP) FOR CONSERVATION AND MANAGEMENT OF PALLIKARANAI MARSH

Out of the 233 respondents, 170 (73%) respondents are WTP for the conservation and management of the marsh whereas 63 respondents (27%) were NWTP for the conservation and management of the marsh (Table 6.5.1, Figure 6.5.1. It was seen earlier that when the question was asked to the respondents whether they were ready to save the marsh, all the respondents agreed to save the marsh. When the respondents were asked as to whether they are WTP for the conservation of the marsh, only 170 respondents were WTP and 63 respondents refused to pay even though they were willing to save the marsh. This shows that even though the people around the marsh are aware of the deteriorating water quality shrinking of the marsh, they were NWTP monetarily, hence the difference in the respondents' opinion on saving the marsh and WTP for the conservation of the marsh.

From the Table 6.5.2 and Figure 6.5.2, it is seen that out of 73 respondents who were men, 52 (71%) were WTP and 21 (29%) were Not Willing to Pay (NWTP) whereas respondents who were women, out of 160, 118 (74%) were WTP and 42 (26%) were Not Willing to Pay. Thus, more are WTP for the conservation of the Pallikaranai Marsh.

It is seen from the above para, out of 63 (21 men and 42 women) NWTP, 40 respondents (17%) stated that the government should pay for the conservation and management of the marsh, whereas 23 respondents (10%) stated that their income was not sufficient, hence were unable to pay for the conservation of marsh. These respondents were willing to save the marsh but financially were not able to help in the conservation of the marsh. (Table 6.5.3, Figure 6.5.3)

The maximum amount of WTP per year was examined using the open-ended (WTP) method. The WTP summary reveals that 18% of the respondents are WTP up to Rs. 100/- while a majority (42%) are WTP between Rs. 100/- to Rs. 200/-, and 40% are WTP Rs. 200/- to Rs. 300/-(Table 6.5.4, Figure 6.5.4) **The average WTP for all the 233 respondents is Rs. 99.21 per year.**

Table 6.5.5 and Figure 6.5.5 gives the average willingness to pay (WTP) by gender. Although more women are WTP, the average WTP is Rs. 98/- less compared to that of men (Rs. 102/-). The average WTP for each location is estimated and presented in Table 6.5.6. Estimated WTP by the residents of sample area using the above estimates on the average WTP per year by the respondents will have estimated the WTP by all households in the sample area are reported in Table 6.5.6

▼ **Table 6.5.6:** Willingness to Pay Per Year By the Residents of the Study Area

S. No	Area	Average WTP per year (a)	Total number of households (b)	WTP (a) X (b) (Rupees/year)
1.	Rajesh Nagar	101.38	800	81104.00
2.	Balaji Nagar	53.28	4204	223989.12
3.	Quaide Milliath Nagar	111.86	124	13870.64
4.	Kamatchi Nagar	135.75	369	50091.75
5.	Maposi Nagar	145.48	567	82470.15
	GRAND TOTAL			**4,51,542.67**

The estimates show that Balaji Nagar residents are WTP the highest amount of Rs. 2,23,989 per year followed by the Maposi Nagar residents of Rs. 82,470. The total amount of WTP is Rs. 4,51,542 per year by the residents of five locations.

▼ **Table 6.5.7:** Willing to Pay By the Residents Within 5 Km of Study Area

S. No	Average WTP per year (a)	Total number of households within 5 km of study area (b)	Total WTP (a) X (b) (Rupees / year)
1.	Rs. 99.21	15400	Rs. 15,27,834.00 or Rs. 15 lakhs

The residents close to Pallikaranai Marsh are WTP Rs. 15 lakhs per year. If we extend the area to a 10-15 km radius the amount to be WTP will be substantial.

▼ **Table 6.5.1:** Willingness to Pay for the Conservation and Management of the Pallikaranai Marsh

Willingness to pay to conserve the Marsh	Number of Respondents	Percentage
NO	63	27
YES	170	73
GRAND TOTAL	233	100

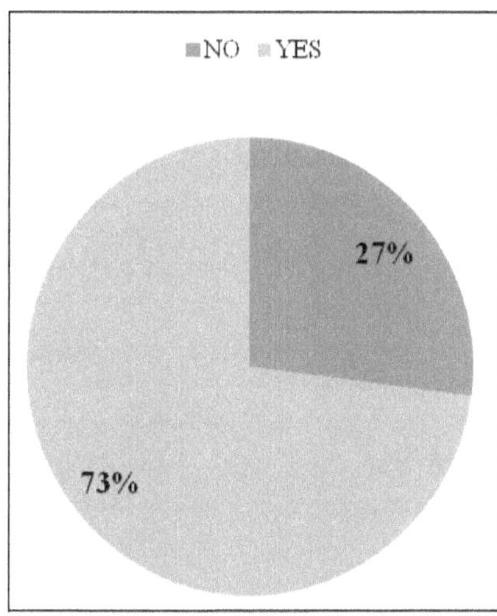

▲ **Figure 6.5.1:** Willingness to Pay for the Conservation and Management of the Pallikaranai Marsh

▼ **Table 6.5.2:** Opinion of the Respondents on the Conservation and Management of the Pallikaranai Marsh

Opinion of the Respondents	Number of Respondents		Number of Respondents		
	men	Percentage	women	Percentage	Total
Willingness to Pay	52	71	118	74	170
Not Willing to Pay	21	29	42	26	63
	73	100	160	100	233

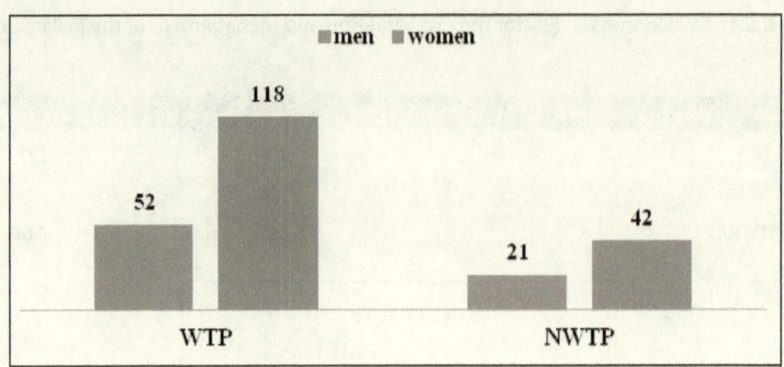

▲ **Figure 6.5.2:** Opinion of the Respondents on the Conservation and Management of the Pallikaranai Marsh

▼ **Table 6.5.3:** Opinion of the Respondents for Not Willing to Pay (nwtp) for the Conservation of Pallikaranai Marsh

Opinion of the Respondents	Number of Respondents	*Percentage*
WTP	170	73
NWTP-government to pay	40	17
NWTP-income insufficient	23	10
Grand total	**233**	**100**

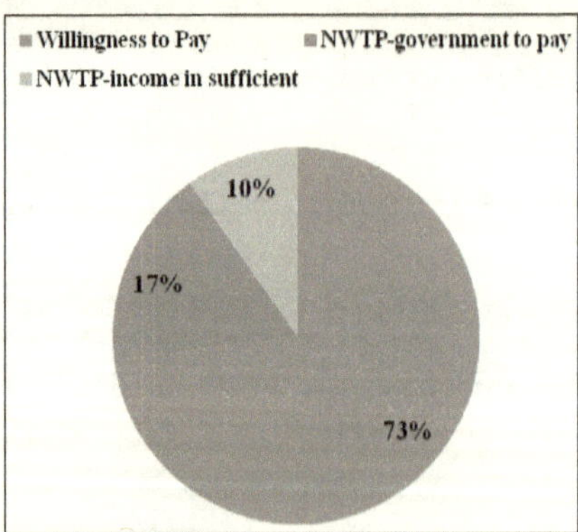

▲ **Figure 6.5.3:** Opinion of the Respondents for Not Willing to Pay for the Conservation of Pallikaranai Marsh

▼ **Table 6.5.4:**   Maximum Willingness to Pay By the Respondents

Maximum WTP	Number of respondents	Percentage
1-100	35	18
101-200	98	42
200-300	37	13
TOTAL	**233**	**100**

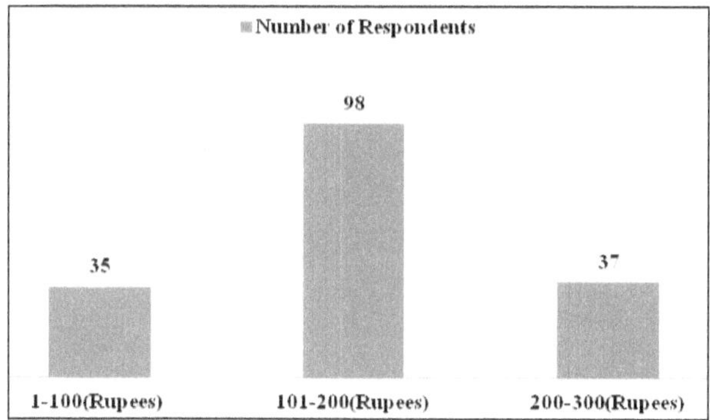

▲ **Figure 6.5.4:**   Maximum Willingness to Pay By Respondents

▼ **Table 6.5.5:**   Average Willingness to Pay Value in Rupees / Year

Respondents (men/women)	Average Willingness to Pay Value in rupees/year
MEN	**101.94**
WOMEN	**98.11**

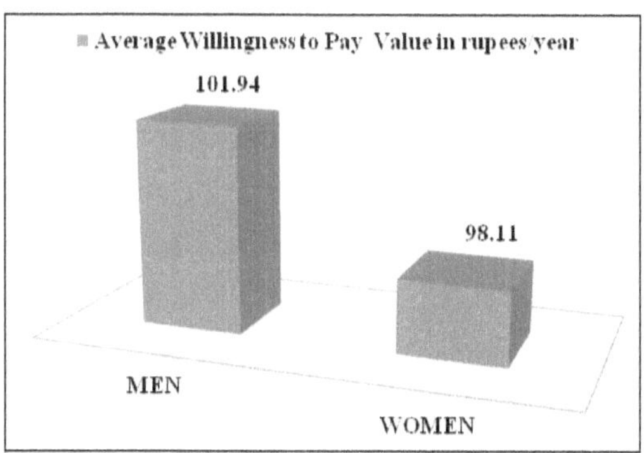

▲ **Figure 6.5.5:**   Average Willingness to Pay Value in Rupees / Year

Source: Based on the data compiled and analyzed by the Author

Contingent Valuation (CV) Analysis

The factors influencing the decision regarding WTP and the amount a respondent is willing to pay per year for the conservation of the Pallikaranai Marsh is analyzed using the following multivariate regression model:

$$WTP = \beta_0 + \beta_2 (Age)_i + \beta_3 (Age\ square)_i + \beta_4 (sex)_i + \beta_5 (Primary)_i + \beta_6 (Secondary)_i + \beta_7 (HSC\text{-}Above)_i + \beta_8 (Family\ Size)_i + \beta_9 (hh\ Income)_i + \beta_{10} (Distance)_i + \beta_{11} (Yrs\text{-}staying)_i + u_i$$

where β_1 are parameters to be estimated and u is the random disturbance term.

The dependent variable WTP is the stated willingness to pay for the conservation of the Pallikaranai Marsh by the respondents. It is measured in two ways, as a dichotomous variable which takes the value of one if the respondent is WTP and zero otherwise, and the amount willing to pay per annum in rupees

The independent variables chosen for the analysis are based on earlier works using CVM namely Bandyopathyay et al (2005), in the context of urban wetlands of Kolkata region, Hadker et al (1997), for Borivli National Park, and Imandoust and Gadan (2007), for Pavana river in Pune.

The most important determinant observed in the literature in CV analysis is the **income** of the respondents or family. The income of the family is the household income per month in Indian rupee. As the income increases, the household's ability to pay will be more and the households will spend more on other than basic necessities. It is expected to have a positive influence on WTP decisions.

The **age** (in years) of the respondents is included as one of the control variables and its square term is also included to capture the non-linearity in the age effect on WTP.

The **education** of the respondent is a dummy variable – primary, secondary, and above. The reference group is below primary which includes illiterates. The education variable is expected to capture the information and knowledge of the adverse impact of the environmental impact of the marsh. The two education dummy variables are expected to positively affect WTP.

The **distance** (in km) measures the distance of the household from the marsh and it is expected to have a positive effect on WTP. The number of years of residence in the area is expected to have a positive effect on WTP.

The **family-related variables** namely the number of family members (family size), number of dependents, number of earning members in the family are also included. As these variables are highly correlated, only family size is included in the final estimates. The family size is expected to have a negative effect on WTP.

▼ **Table 6.5.8:** Summary Statistics of Variables Used in WTP Analysis

Variable	Obs	Mena	Standard Deviation	Minimum	Maximum
Dependent variables					
Willing to Pay (Rupees / year) All	233	99.21	77.21	0	254
Willingness to Pay (only those WTP)	170	135.97	56.167	54	254
Willing to Pay (Yes / No)	233	0.7253	0.4473	0	1
Independent variables					
Age of the respondent (in years)	233	39.931	12.523	14	85
Age Square (in years)	233	1750.7	1103.2	196	7225
Gender (Male =1, Female=0)	233	0.279	0.4495	0	1
Education of the Respondent					
Completed Primary Level	233	0.2017	0.4021	0	1
Completed Secondary Level	233	0.4549	0.499	0	1
Completed Higher Secondary & Above	233	0.103	0.3046	0	1
Number of dependents	233	0.6567	1.2257	0	9
Number of Working members	233	1.5794	0.7034	1	4
Family size	233	4.3562	1.6524	1	14
Household Income (Rupees / month)	233	4657.5	2137.9	700	15000
Years living in the area	233	13.779	8.0215	1	47
Distance to the Marsh	233	0.518	0.0997	0.4	0.7

Source: Computed using the CV primary survey data

The summary statistics of the variables used in the CV survey of 233 respondents are given in Table 6.5.8. The average age of the respondent is about 40 years and the average family income for a family size of 4.35 members is Rs. 4657 per month. On average there are about 1.68 working members in a family. The average distance of households from Pallikaranai Marsh is about half a kilometer and these families have been residing for about 13.78 years. The survey thus reveals that households are located close to the Pallikaranai Marsh. They have been long time residents in the study region and are poor. Going by the current definition of the poverty line of an average of Rs. 66 per capita per day (The Hindu April 29, 2012) for urban, the residents in the study region are below the poverty line.

Estimation Method

In the analysis, the WTP consists of two parts. The first is the decision on whether the respondent is willing to pay or not (dichotomous choice decision) and the second stage consists of the amount willing to pay if the respondent willing to pay. for the conservation of the marsh. Based on this, the model is formulated and the estimation method is discussed below:

First, the WTP is treated as a dichotomous choice decision and the factors influencing WTP are examined. In the case of a dichotomous variable, the ordinary least squares (OLS) method leads to inconsistent and inefficient estimates, It also results in the econometric problem such as heteroscedasticity, and further, the predicted probability may not lie with the 0-1 interval. Hence we estimate the model using both maximum likelihood logit and probit methods. For comparison and to check whether the two non-linear methods – logit and probit – leads to any unrealistic estimates, we also present the OLS estimates.

Second, the determinants of the amount a respondent is willing to pay per annum restricting to only those who willing to pay are examined. The model is called **conditional WTP model** and this can be estimated by the OLS method.

Alternatively, we can pool all samples (those who are WTP and those who are not WTP) and setting the amount paid by those who are NWTP as zero the model can be estimated by the **Generalized Tobit method**. This merges the two decisions – WTP and the amount willing to pay.

All three methods are applied and the results are presented and discussed in the following section.

Empirical Results and Discussion

The estimates of the determinants of the WTP by OLS, logit, and probit methods are given in Table 6.5.9. In the logit and probit models, the marginal effects are computed based on the estimates and also reported. The marginal effects are comparable to the OLS estimates but their standard errors are not. The findings from the three methods of estimation are more or less the same. The age and its square term and gender do not exert a statistically significant effect event at a 10% level. An important factor that influences the diction on the WTP is education. The coefficient of the dummy variables of secondary and higher secondary and above levels of education are positive and also statistically significant in all the models.

▼ **Table 6.5.9:** Estimates of the Determinants of WTP By OLS, Probit, and Logit Methods (Dependent variable: WTP Dichotomous variable (yes =1, no=0))

Explanatory Variable	OLS		Probit			Logit		
	Coefficient	t'	Coefficient	Marginal Effect	t' Value	Coefficient	Marginal Effect	t' value
Age of the respondent (in years)	-0.0158	-1.22	-0.0546	-0.0174	-1.3	-0.0943	-0.0174	-1.24
Age Square (in years)	0.00017	1.15	0.00057	0.00018	1.24	0.00099	0.00018	1.18
Gender (Male =1, Female=0)	-0.0759	-1.13	-0.2145	-0.0703	-0.99	-0.395	-0.076	-1.05
Completed Primary Level	-0.0205	-0.24	-0.1	-0.0324	-1.38	-0.1376	-0.0259	-0.31
Completed Secondary Level	0.16084	2.15	0.4957	0.15456	2.05	0.84902	0.15301	2.14
Completed Higher Secondary & Above	0.20663	3.05	0.02471	0.2781	3.07	0.09252	0.1873	2.15
Family size	-0.01907	-2.06	0.06932	-0.02206	-2.08	0.10644	-0.01962	-1.96
Household Income (Rupees/month)	0.00032	2.73	0.00012	0.00039	2.82	0.00021	0.00038	2.14
Years Living in the Area	0.037	2.10	0.051	0.022	2.12	0.0021	0.041	2.10
Distance to the Marsh	-0.62431	-1.99	-1.81867	-0.57883	-1.74	-3.41884	-0.6302	-1.88
Constant	0.45679	1.46	-0.0977		-0.1	-0.2568		-0.14
R-square/Psuedo R-Square	0.08		0.10			0.11		
Log-Likelihood ratio			-122.64			-122.45		
# of Observations	233		233			233		

Note: 't' values in parentheses
Source: Computed using the CV primary survey data

This suggests that the respondents with secondary and higher secondary and above levels of education are more likely to pay for conservation than their counterparts namely persons with primary or less than primary levels of education. The sign of the coefficient of the income of the respondent's family is positive and the effect is statistically significant at a 1% level. The results suggest that one thousand rupees increase in the income of the family is likely to increase livelihood that the respondent is willing to pay by 3-4% . The distance of the household from the marsh and the duration of residence in the locality have a positive effect and these effects are statistically significant at 5%. The results suggest that the closer the residence to the marsh, the more likely the resident to pay for conservation of the marsh, and persons staying in the locality for a longer period are also more likely to pay for the conservation. One kilometer increase in the distance from the marsh, the probability the resident will be willing to pay will reduce by 0.60. That is the chances of paying for conservation increase to 60% if the resident is 1 km closer to the marsh. Similarly, one year increase in living in the area will increase the probability of willing to pay by 0.02-0.03. In other words, one year increase in the years of stay, the chances of WTP will increase by 2-3%. This clearly indicates that the distance is an important factor in the determination of the WTP.

The conditional WTP model estimated by OLS and the WTP estimated by the Generalized Tobit method are given in Table 6.5.10. The estimates of the **Conditional WTP model** given in column 2-3 of Table 6.5.10 suggest that only the coefficient of the variables namely age square family income, higher secondary and above levels of education exert a statistically significant (at 10% level) effect while the effect of other variables is not statistically significant. This suggests that the amount the households are WTP depends on income and higher levels of education while the decision to pay is influenced by several factors as discussed above. The effects of age and its square term indicate that the amount willing to pay decreases at an increasing rate as the age of the respondent increases. The effect of gender turns out to be statistically insignificant at a 10% level which implies that there is a gender-specific difference in the amount willing to pay by the respondents.

▼ Table 6.5.10:   Estimates of the Determinants of the WTP By OLS and Generalized Tobit Methods

Explanatory variable	Conditional WTP (Respondents who are willing to pay)		Willingness to Pay (All respondents)			
	OLS		OLS		Generalized Tobit	
	Coefficient	t'	Coefficient	t' value	Coefficient	t' value
Age of the respondent (in years)	-3.556434	-1.1	-0.09933	-0.04	-0.83416	-1.58
Age Square (in years)	0.04015	-1.63	0.000771	0.03	0.008269	0.25
Gender (Male =1, Female=0)	9.317329	0.88	2.912089	0.25	-1.05433	-0.07
Completed Primary Level	8.640322	0.6	5.425526	0.37	9.961647	0.5
Completed Secondary Level	0.840587	0.97	23.5314	2.83	37.80052	2.19
Completed Higher Secondary & Above	1.60177	2.19	1.7319	2.92	4.386069	3.17
Family size	3.042954	1.1	4.338772	2.40	5.709534	2.4
Household Income (Rupees/month)	0.0466	2.92	0.08033	5.17	0.010099	5.07
Years Living in the Area	-0.11371	-0.21	1.01754	1.82	0.06198	1.77
Distance to the Marsh	-8.404165	-0.17	-91.21155	-3.69	-144.4489	-3.044
Constant	23.69881	0.45	-14.5018	-0.27	-0.2568	-0.89
R-square / Pseudo R-square	0.14		0.36		0.34	
Log-Likelihood Ratio				-1074.54		
# of observations	170		233		233	

Note: 't' values in parentheses
Source: Computed using the CV primary survey data

The **OLS and Generalized Tobit** estimates are given in 4-7 in Table 6.5.10. It should be noted that the effect of the decision to pay or not and the amount to be paid once the respondent decides to pay are captured in this model. As observed in the case of the dichotomous choice model, the important determinants are education, income, distance to the Marsh, the number of years living in the area, and family. The coefficients of these variables are statistically significant at 5% or above. The estimates suggest that a thousand rupees increase in the household income per month will increase the amount the respondent willing to pay increases by Rupees 80 per year. The respondents with secondary and higher secondary & above levels of education are willing to pay Rupees 3 more than the illiterate or primary educated respondents. The results of this study show that there is no gender difference in the WTP for the conservation of the Marsh. The families living closer to Marshland by one kilometer are willing to pay Rupees 91 more than their counterparts who are living one kilometer away from the Marsh. One additional member in the family increases the WTP by Rs. 4. People who are staying for a longer period of time are willing to pay Re 1 for every additional year of stay.

The important findings emerging from the CV method can be summarized as follows: The people living in the sample area are below the poverty line and in many of the households about two persons work to earn their livelihood. The multivariate analysis reveals that the income of the families is an important factor in influencing the decision to pay as well as the amount willing to pay to conserve the Pallikaranai Marsh. The education of the respondent enhances the ability to gather and understand the information relevant to social issues. The multivariate analysis reveals that secondary and above levels of education are necessary to understand the environmental issues and those with secondary and above are willing to pay for the conservation of Pallikaranai Marsh. People near the marsh are more affected than those living away from the marshland. The econometric analysis reveals that distance is an important factor that influences the decision as well as the amount WTP. Similarly, people living in that locality for a longer duration are more exposed to the harmful effects of environmental degradation and they are willing to pay more than people who have become residents in recent years.

The socio-economic conditions of the respondents are almost the same. They are from the lower middle class. They feel the environmental problems that are prevailing in the Pallikaranai Marsh. They are also aware of the environmental problems and other problems prevailing in Chennai city. It is seen that environmental problems including quality drinking water are the major and very important problem for the respondents. They feel that in spite of living very close to the wetland, they are not able to utilize the water in the marsh as most of them rate the water as 'Worst.' The move made by the Forest department to fence the area of 317.00 Ha of wetland and conserve the area was very much appreciated by the respondents. They have also welcomed the idea of conservation and management of Pallikaranai Marsh but they think that they are poor and there is nobody to voice their message.

When the respondents were asked as to whether they are WTP for the conservation of the marsh, only 170 respondents were WTP and 63 respondents refused to pay even though they were willing to save the marsh. This shows that even though the people around the marsh are aware of the deteriorating water quality, shrinking of the marsh, they were NWTP monetarily, hence the difference in the respondents' opinion on saving the marsh and WTP for the conservation of the marsh.

The maximum amount of WTP per year was examined using the open-ended (WTP) method. The average WTP for all the 233 respondents is Rs. 99.21 per year. The estimates show that Balaji Nagar residents are WTP the highest amount of Rs. 2,23,989 per year followed by the Maposi Nagar residents of Rs. 82,470. The total amount of WTP is Rs. 4,51,542 per year by the residents of five locations. The residents close to Pallikaranai Marsh (within 5kms) are WTP Rs. 15 lakhs per year. If we extend the area to a 10-15 km radius the amount to be WTP will be substantial.

The average age of the respondent is about 40 years and the average family income for a family size of 4.35 members is Rs. 4657 per month.

The results suggest that one thousand rupees increase in the income of the family is likely to increase livelihood that the respondent is WTP by 3-4%. One year increase in living in the area will increase the probability of WTP by 0.02-0.03. In other words, one year increase in the years of stay, the chances of WTP will increase by 2-3%. The analysis reveals that the distance is an important factor which influences the decision as well as the amount WTP.

SUMMARY, CONCLUSIONS, LIMITATIONS AND POLICY SUGGESTIONS

The study on the changes in land use/land cover in Pallikaranai Marsh between 1991 to 2010 is analyzed and it is seen that the area under the wetland and grassland has decreased, whereas the area under the settlements and dump yard has increased tremendously between 1991 to 2010. It is seen that the increase in the settlements is from 138 ha in 1991 to 1146 ha in 2010. Due to the rapid urbanization, the waste generated in the major part of Chennai city is being dumped in the marsh; as a result, the marsh has witnessed an increase in dump area by 60.37 ha. The STP in the marsh area was under operation from 2006 under the CCRCP scheme; hence in the year 2010, 23.52 ha was under the STP. There was a rapid decrease in grassland from 1424.02 ha in 1991 to 401.38 ha in the year 2010.

The land use pattern for the year 1991 and 2010 respectively shows that there is a significant increase in settlements, which increased from 138 ha in 1991 to 1146.28 ha in 2010. Due to rapid urbanization in the Velachery area and also due to the waste generated in the major part of the Chennai city being dumped inside the marsh (in Perungudi dump yard), the marsh has clearly witnessed an increase in dump area by 91.22% between the year 1990 to 2010. A rapid decrease in the area of grassland from 1424.02 to 401.38 ha in 2010 indicated that human activities strengthened the disturbance of wetland.

The analysis of the water quality in the Pallikaranai Marsh is detailed, including the relationship between wetlands and water quality in general. The deterioration of water quality is mainly due to the dump yard in the Pallikaranai Marsh. The study area, the methodology of collection of water samples and analyzing them for pH, EC, total hardness, sodium, potassium, nitrate, sulfate, and fluoride, chlorides, total dissolved solids BOD, COD, heavy metals like copper, zinc, iron, lead, nickel, cadmium, chromium, and manganese are presented and discussed. The dug wells and the tube wells locations were within 2 km from the Perungudi dump yard in Pallikaranai Marsh. The determination of the quality of groundwater around a Perungudi dump yard in Pallikaranai and its adjacent area in the thirteen dug wells, nine tube wells, and four surface water samples were established as observation wells in the pre-monsoon and post-monsoon periods in June 2008, January 2009, June 2009 and January 2010 and to compare it with the water quality standards by CPHEEO (1999) was presented and discussed. Thereafter, to compare COD, BOD and heavy metals in the water samples in six observation wells in the same location both in dug wells and tube wells for pre and post-monsoon periods from June 2008 to January 2010 was presented and discussed.

Groundwater samples were collected in two seasons of pre-monsoon and post-monsoon for a period of two years (June 2008 to January 2010) from13 dug wells, nine tube wells, and four surface water samples from

Pallikaranai Marsh and Okkiyam Madugu were collected surrounding the dumping yard.

For heavy metal analysis, separate samples were collected; after the collection of the water samples, the samples were acidified immediately with 1:1 Hydrochloric acid. Similarly, separate samples were collected for BOD and COD analysis. The samples were immediately transported to the laboratory and carefully stored for analysis in the TWAD Board, Chennai.

The samples were analyzed for relevant physio-chemical parameters such as pH, total dissolved solids, electrical conductivity, total hardness, calcium, magnesium, sodium, potassium, BOD, COD, carbonate, bicarbonate, chloride, fluoride, nitrate, sulfate and heavy metals like iron, copper, cadmium, zinc, manganese, chromium, nickel, and lead. pH & EC was measured in the field immediately after the collection of water samples. All the parameters were analyzed following the procedure specified in APHA (1998). pH, EC, sodium, potassium, nitrate, sulfate, chloride, and fluoride were analyzed in the instrumental method. Total hardness, calcium, magnesium, carbonate, bicarbonate, and chloride were analyzed in the titrimetric method. All the heavy metals were analyzed in the atomic absorption spectrophotometric method. In the study area, the groundwater is used for domestic and other purposes. All the samples were analyzed Water Analysis Laboratory in the TWAD Board, Chennai.

The pH of the dug wells, tube wells, and surface water varies from 6.75 to 8.12. The EC in the pre-monsoon period varies from 536 to 7254µS /cm and in the post-monsoon period the EC varies from 632 to 6102 µS /cm. the TDS in the pre-monsoon period varies from 697mg/l to 5306 mg/l with an average of 3162 mg/l in dug wells, 4114 mg/l in tube wells, and 2821 mg/l in surface water. During the pre-monsoon period, the total hardness is generally high in dug wells, tube wells, and surface water (varies from 141-1249) than in the post-monsoon period (varies from 42 to 1120).

The calcium content varies from 9-386 mg/l in the pre-monsoon periods for the dug wells, tube wells, and surface water. Similarly, it varies between 22-237 mg/l in the post-monsoon period. The magnesium content in the pre-monsoon is between 9-168 mg/l and the post-monsoon period is between 9-168 mg/l. in dug wells, tube wells, and surface water. The sodium content in the pre-monsoon periods varies from 18-1362 mg/l and in the post-monsoon periods varies from 24-1355 mg/l. The concentration of potassium varies from 5-203 mg/l in both pre-monsoon and post-monsoon periods, in groundwater, and surface water. The concentration of sulfate in the water samples during the pre-monsoon period varies from 26-069 mg/l and in the post-monsoon period varies from 26-1018 mg/l. The bicarbonates in the pre-monsoon period vary from 148-1747 mg/l, whereas in the post-monsoon period it varies from 137-1290 mg/l for dug wells, tube wells, and surface water.

The chloride content during the pre-monsoon period for groundwater and surface water varied from 97-2285 mg/l and in the post-monsoon period, it varied from 119-1531 mg/l. The fluoride content varies from 0.23 to 1.71 mg/l during the pre-monsoon period and 0.60 to 1.51 mg/l during the post-monsoon period. Nitrate content during the pre-monsoon period for the groundwater and surface water varied from 9.82 to 421.80 mg/l and in post-monsoon varied from 5.97 to 177.84 mg/l.

The COD value varies from 20- 276 mg/l in the pre-monsoon period and 25-129 mg/l during the post-monsoon period, whereas BOD values vary from 6.2 to 155 in the pre-monsoon period for dug wells, tube wells, and surface water. The BOD is lower in the post-monsoon season and varied from 5.8 to 127 mg/l. It was found that the minimum and maximum content of heavy metals in pre and post-monsoon seasons from June 2008 to January 2010 in all wells were copper (BDL-0.55mg/l), iron (0.01-2.49 mg/l) and Zinc (BDL-0.67mg/l), lead (BDL-0.10mg/l), nickel, (BDL-0.38mg/l), manganese (BDL-0.86mg/l) and chromium (BDL-0.023 mg/l) and cadmium (BDL-0.11mg/l).

The seasonal variation was analyzed and discussed for BOD, COD, and heavy metal values in dug wells and tube wells during June 2008, January 2009, June 2009 and January 2010 from the same locations. On analyzing the values of the various physico-chemical parameters for the different seasons in thirteen dug wells, nine tube wells, and four surface water samples, it is seen that the pH exhibits alkaline nature in all the water samples. The EC content in the post-monsoon period reduces due to the rains which dilute the water. In the present study, the TDS in all the water samples was high and exceeded the desired limit of the CPHEEO (1999). In the case of hardness, the values are higher during the pre-monsoon period and exceed the maximum allowable limit. Calcium, magnesium, potassium, sodium sulfate, bicarbonate values are higher in the pre-monsoon period than in the post-monsoon periods due to dilution that takes place during rains. The nitrate is higher in the pre-monsoon periods and in chloride, fluoride, and nitrate the values in the water samples exceed the desirable level by CPHEEO (1999).

Both in the case of COD and BOD, the values are higher in pre-monsoon and lower in the post-monsoon period. In the case of heavy metals, the average lead content in the water samples was above the desirable limits of CPHEEO (1999), both in pre and post-monsoon periods. A similar pattern was seen in copper, nickel, iron, and manganese. These values in the water sample are below the desirable limit of CPHEEO (1999), in the case of zinc. Cadmium and chromium content in the water samples are within the desirable values of CPHEEO (1999), and only in locations close to the dump yard, the levels were above the desirable level.

In the study undertaken on the seasonal variation for BOD and COD values in dug wells and tube wells during June 2008, January 2009, June 2009, and January 2010 from the same locations, the results are: the COD values in the dug wells during the pre-monsoon and post-monsoon periods in June 2008, January 2009, June 2008 and January 2010 show that the pre-monsoon values are higher than the post-monsoon values. The COD values in Thuraipakkam-Shanmugam and Perungudi-Elumalai House is high as they are close to the dump yard. Whereas, the values in the location Mettukuppam Pillaiyar Koil street is low as it away from the dump yard. The COD values in the tube wells during the pre-monsoon and post-monsoon periods in June 2008, January 2009, June 2009 and January 2010 show that the pre-monsoon values are higher than the post-monsoon values and is highest in the location Thuraipakkam-Jayabalan and is closer to the dump yard. The values in the location Mettukuppam Pillaiyarkoil street is low both in pre-monsoon and post-monsoon season as the location is away from the dump yard. A similar trend was seen in the dug wells values for COD.

The BOD values in the dug wells during the pre-monsoon and post-monsoon season show that the values are higher in the pre-monsoon periods than the post-monsoon period. The values in pre-monsoon and post-monsoon periods were high in all the locations closer to the dumpsite; except in Thuraipakkam-Adiparasakthi K. M. is slightly low as it is a little away from the dumpsite and low in the location Mettukuppam Pillayar Koil street, which is away from the dump yard. In the tube wells data for BOD, the trend is similar to the case of the dug wells. The BOD values in the tube wells during the pre-monsoon and post-monsoon were studied during June 2008, January 2009, June 2009 and January 2010 and they show that the values are higher in the pre-monsoon period than the post-monsoon period.

In the study undertaken on the seasonal variation for heavy metal values in dug wells and tube wells during June 2008, January 2009, June 2009 and January 2010 from the same locations, the results are the average copper content in the water sample was high during the post-monsoon period and this is due to the solubility and mobility in the landfill site and migration of contaminants from the dump yard. For the average lead content, the post-monsoon values are higher than the pre-monsoon values in all the cases. With respect to the average zinc content, the post-monsoon values were higher than the pre-monsoon values in all the cases. The iron content in the pre-monsoon season was higher in the dug wells and tube wells than the post-monsoon period in all the locations. In the case of average manganese content, the pre-monsoon values were higher in all locations when compared to post-monsoon values due to the dilution of metal in post-monsoon.

The EC content in the post-monsoon period reduces due to the rains which dilute the water. In the present study, the TDS in all the water samples were high and exceeded the desired limit of the CPHEEO, (1999). In the case of hardness, the values are higher during the pre-monsoon period and exceed the maximum allowable limit. Calcium, magnesium, potassium, sodium, sulfate, and bicarbonate values are higher in the pre-monsoon period than in the post-monsoon periods due to dilution that takes place during rains. The nitrate is higher in the pre-monsoon periods and in chlorides, fluorides, and nitrates the values in the water samples exceed the desirable level by CPHEEO, (1999).

COD and BOD: Both in the case of COD and BOD, the water sample are higher in pre-monsoon and lower in the post-monsoon period.

In the case of heavy metals, the average lead content in the in the water samples is above the desirable limits of CPHEEO (1999), both in pre and post-monsoon periods. A similar pattern was seen in copper, nickel, iron, and manganese. The water sample values are below the desirable limit of CPHEEO (1999), in the case of zinc. Cadmium and chromium content in the water samples are within the desirable values of CPHEEO (1999), and only in locations close to the dump yard the levels were above the desirable level.

Wetlands provide many important services to human society but are at the same time ecologically sensitive systems. The services provided by wetlands include habitat for species, protection against floods, water purification, amenities, and recreational opportunities. Because these services typically have no market price, a measure of their values can only be obtained through non-market valuation techniques. Many wetland valuation studies have been conducted and the range of the estimates is remarkable.

In the economic valuation methods, CVM uses surveys of expressed preferences to evaluate WTP for (generally) non-market, environmental goods. This approach gives the method, in theory, wide applicability to an extensive range of use and passive-use values associated with such goods. Only one known valuation approach, CVM, can in principle provide useful information about the economic significance of lost passive-use values when ecosystems are degraded or destroyed by pollution and/or development. The open-ended approach in CVM is convenient to answer, does not require an interviewer, and does not result in any starting point bias.

Although entire South Chennai is affected by the environmental degradation and dumping of garbage in the Pallikaranai Marshland, it is not possible to collect data from all localities due to the time and cost constraints of an individual researcher. Moreover, there is no household-level survey data available from secondary sources to study the socio-economic conditions of the population in and around Pallikaranai Marsh. Hence, it was decided to confirm the study area within one kilometer in and around of Pallikaranai Marsh area. People residing in these localities are more affected due to environmental degradation than areas away from the Marsh There are several residential localities, consisting of one to two streets, called with different prefixes, like Nagar. There are localities within the radius of one kilometer and five localities are selected residential localities (in local government it is called wards) as a simple random sample method.

The selected wards are Balaji Nagar, Kamakshi Nagar, Rajesh Nagar, Ma. Po. Si. Nagar and Quaide Millaith Nagar. A list of households in each of these localities was prepared. A random sample of 20% of households was selected at random using a simple random sampling method. Before the main survey, the pre-testing of the interview schedule was undertaken in the area. The draft interview schedule was prepared prior to pre-testing, which consisted of three major parts. In this study, the first round of pre-testing was done in the month of November 2008 for a period of six days and the second round of pre-testing was done in the month of January 2009, for a period of 15 days. The inputs from the first round of pre-testing were used to improve the overall structure of the interview schedule. The purpose of the second round was to strengthen the contingent valuation scenarios as well as some of the other aspects of the remaining contingent valuation component.

During the initial survey, the potential biases that we initially encountered in the field was the interviewer bias. When we initially went around the study area, the households treated us like *outsiders*. Later we started speaking in the local language i. e., Tamil for which they felt comfortable. We had taken the help of the local self-help group ladies, who volunteered to come with us to interact with the respondent initially. The respondents were asked to answer all the questions in the interview schedule and were asked to state their own preferences on all aspects in an open-ended way. In the present study, commodity valued is the conservation of the wetland for quality drinking water. The respondent may consider for the conservation of the Pallikaranai Marsh in order to get quality drinking water in future. In this study, all the respondents were aware of the environmental problems in the marsh, they were willing to save the marsh and hence no protest bid is seen. The payment vehicle here was an 'Annual fee' for conserving the Pallikaranai Marsh for quality drinking water and the respondents were informed that they would pay the amount every year.

The final survey was conducted from July to September 2009. The household interview was conducted among the adult members of the sample households who were above 18 years old. However, only one member was requested to answer all the questions in the interview schedule, but consultation with the other household members was allowed.

It is seen that out of the total respondent of 233, 166 (71%) respondents are women and 67 (29%) respondents are men. There were more women who were ready to come forward as they felt the need to get quality drinking water. All the respondents belong to the age group above 18 years and below 70 years.

Out of the 233 households, nearly 66% (153) of the households are found to be living in this area for less than 25 years, 23% (54) of households are found to be living in this area for about 25-50 years and 11%(26) households are living here for >50 years.

The family size of the households of the respondents ranges from 1 to 14 numbers. Out of the 233 households, 78 (33%) of households live in a family of four and 59 (25%) of households live in a family of five. Nineteen households only live in a family size of more than seven members. Three respondents have a family size of 9, 11, and 14.

The educational qualification of the respondents reveals that the 56 (24%) respondents are uneducated and have not received any formal education. 106 (45%) respondents have studied between 6-10th standard. There are only four professionals out of the total number of respondents. It is also seen that 20 (9%) respondents have studied >10th standard.

The income range of the men and women respondents shows that the 42 of the respondents who are women have no income. 139 respondents have an income range of up to Rs. 3500/. Out of 139 respondents, 105 are women and 34 are men. 42 respondents have an income between Rs. 3500 to 7,500. Of which, 23 are men and 19 are women. It is seen that the income earned by ten male respondents is >Rs. 7500/-. Most of the men and women respondents have a low income which is up to Rs. 3500/. The respondents chosen in this study are generally from a poorer background.

There are only 8 (12%) of the male respondents who are into government jobs and the rest 40 (60%) of the male respondents are self-employed. They are self-employed and are into carpentry, masonry, shopkeeping, etc. 42 women respondents out of 166 are without any occupation. They prefer to stay at home in order to take care of the children and elders and some of them due to health problems stay at home. The study reveals that 100 (61%) respondents who are women are self-employed. They work in petty shops, own small shops, or do some petty works, household work in other nearby flats. 20 (12%) of the respondents work in private companies in the nearby area. It is seen that 121 (52%) respondents have only one member in their households who are employed and 95 respondents (41%) have only two members employed in their households. Similarly, 11 respondents (5%) show three employed and six respondents (2%) show four employed in their respective households. Regarding the source of water in the households for the respondents, most of them use the public tap. Only 16 respondents have individual connections, two respondents have hand pumps, and two respondents have their own well. Two of the respondents informed that there was no water source near their area.

It is seen that 120 (51%) of the respondents have both radio and televisions and 200 (86%) respondents use both cookers and fans in their houses as they are minimum basic needs for themselves. 134 (57%) respondents use motorcycles and nearly 86 (37%) respondents do not own a vehicle.

The opinions of the respondents on the various major problems faced in Chennai and in the Pallikaranai Marsh show that the environmental problems including quality drinking water is the major and very important problem. Nearly 150 respondents, out of 233, opine that this problem was very important. Similarly, as per the opinion of the respondents, education followed by crime than corruption and lastly unemployment were in the order of importance.

It was seen that the solid waste dumping was the most important problem as out of 233 respondents, 170 opine that it was the most important problem. This was followed by sewerage, increasing population, and lastly encroachment.

Out of 233 respondents, 150 (64%) respondents expressed that the water quality of the marsh should be improved. Nearly 40 (18%) respondents have expressed that garbage dumping should be stopped in the marsh to prevent water and air pollution in and around the marsh. Similarly, 36 respondents (15%) expressed that sewerage water should not be allowed in the marsh area. Lastly, seven respondents (3%) opine that encroachment in the marshland is very critical due to which the area of the marsh is shrinking.

Nearly 150 respondents opine that the drinking water is the most important service which they could receive from the Pallikaranai Marsh followed by recreation and tourism (29%), employment to fishermen (4%), and stability of microclimate (2%).

In the present survey, it was seen that 206 (88.5%) respondents are of the opinion that the marsh is highly polluted, 15 (6.5%) opine that the marsh is moderately polluted, and 12 (5%) that it is marginally polluted. It is also seen that 222 (95%) respondents rate the water quality of the marsh as *worst* and 11 (5%) opine that it is *bad*.

Out of the 233 respondents, 170 (73%) respondents are WTP for the conservation and management of the marsh whereas 63 respondents (27%) were NWTP for the conservation and management of the marsh.

It is seen that out of 73 respondents who were men, 52 (71%) were WTP, and 21 (29%) were NWTP whereas respondents who were women, out of 160, 118 (74%) were WTP and 42 (26%) were NWTP. Thus, more are WTP for the conservation of the Pallikaranai Marsh.

Out of 63 (21 men and 42 women) NWTP, 40 respondents (17%) stated that the government should pay for the conservation and management of the marsh, whereas 23 respondents (10%) stated that their income was not sufficient, hence were unable to pay for the conservation of marsh. These respondents were willing to save the marsh but financially were not able to help in the conservation of the marsh.

The average WTP for all the 233 respondents is Rs. 99.21 per year. The average WTP by gender is as follows. Although more women are WTP, the average WTP is Rs. 98/- less compared to that of men (Rs. 102/-). The estimates show that Balaji Nagar residents are WTP the highest amount of Rs. 2,23,989 per year followed by the Maposi Nagar residents of Rs. 82,470. The total amount of WTP is Rs. 4,51,542 per year by the residents of five locations. The residents close to Pallikaranai Marsh are WTP Rs. 15 lakhs per year. If we extend the area to a 10-15 km radius the amount to be WTP will be substantial.

Using multivariate methods (OLS, Probit, and Logit models), the determinants of WTP, and the amount WTP by the respondents are analyzed.

The people living in the sample area are below the poverty line and in many of the households about two persons work to earn their livelihood. The multivariate analysis reveals that the income of the families is an important factor in influencing the decision to pay as well as the amount WTP to conserve the Pallikaranai Marsh. The education of the respondent enhances the ability to gather and understand the information relevant to social issues.

The multivariate analysis reveals that secondary and above levels of education are necessary to understand the environmental issues and those with secondary and above are WTP for the conservation of Pallikaranai Marsh. People near the marsh are more affected than those living away from the marshland.

The econometric analysis reveals that distance is an important factor that influences the decision as well as the amount WTP. Similarly, people living in that locality for a longer duration are more exposed to the harmful effects of environmental degradation and they are WTP more than people who have become residents in recent years.

LIMITATIONS

The comparison in the land use /land cover in Pallikaranai Marsh in the present study for the years 1991 and 2010 was analyzed. Due to cost constraints, the comparison in the land use/ land cover could not be done for the period earlier to the year 1991. In the present study, the physico-chemical analysis including COD, BOD, and heavy metals in water was conducted for the pre and post-monsoon periods from June 2008 to January 2010 in the tube wells and wells within 2 km from the Perungudi dump yard in Pallikaranai Marsh. However, the analysis could not be conducted in dug wells and tube wells within 4 km, 8km, 12km, etc., due to cost, and time constraints.

In the present study, using CVM, 233 respondents were interviewed from five different areas within 1 km from the Perungudi dump yard in Pallikaranai Marsh. This was done as the people residing close to the dump yard are directly affected by the environmental degradation of Pallikaranai Marsh. But comparison could be done with the people who line away from the marsh and are indirectly affected by the degradation of marsh. However, this was not done due to time and budget constraints.

POLICY SUGGESTIONS FOR CONSERVATION AND MANAGEMENT OF PALLIKARANAI MARSH

Wetlands are among the most important ecosystems on earth. Wetlands also have been called *ecological supermarkets* because of the extensive food chain and rich biodiversity that they support. They play major roles in the landscape by providing unique habitats for a wide variety of flora and fauna. Now that we have become concerned about the health of our entire planet, wetlands are being described by some as important carbon sinks and climate stabilizers on a global scale. Scientists, engineers, lawyers and regulators are now finding it both useful and necessary to become specialists in wetland ecology and wetland management in order to understand, preserve, and even reconstruct these fragile ecosystems.

Wetlands are one of the most threatened habitats in the world. According to the UN Millennium Ecosystem Assessment (2005), environmental degradation is more prominent within wetland systems when compared to other natural systems of the earth. This degradation is spread over a range of habitat types that are known under the generic category of wetlands; viz. mangroves, paddy fields, or lakes. The degradation is due to factors such as the process of ill-planned urbanization, industrialization, and encroachments. Wetland ecosystem provides innumerable tangible and intangible benefits to society, but somehow they remain away from the domain of the market forces.

Wetland ecosystems, both inland and coastal, support large biodiversity (flora and fauna). Besides, wetlands yield various products, which give substantial economic returns. To reap these benefits, different types of anthropogenic activities are performed in and around wetlands.

As a consequence, water quality deteriorates, and the habitat is disturbed. Moreover, to derive greater short term, often private benefits, wetlands are often converted to other uses. These conversions not only distort the food chain of the wetland ecosystem but also deprive the beneficiaries who were users of the wetlands.

Valuation is only one element in the effort to improve the management of environmental resources such as wetlands. At the same time, decision-makers must take account of many competing interests in deciding how best to use wetlands. Economic valuation may help inform such management decisions, but only if decision-makers are aware of the overall objectives and limitations of valuation. Therefore the valuation of wetlands is very much needed to save and protect the fragile ecosystem.

The economic valuation is an attempt to assign quantitative values to the goods and services provided by environmental resources, whether or not market prices are available to assist us. The economic value of any good or service is generally measured in terms of what we are willing to pay for the commodity, less what it costs to supply it. Where an environmental resource simply exists and provides us with products and services at no cost, then it is our WTP alone which describes the value of the resource in providing such commodities, whether, or not we actually make any payment.

The main objective of valuation in assisting wetland management decisions is generally to indicate the overall *economic efficiency* of the various competing uses of wetland resources. Thus a wetland use showing a substantial net benefit would be deemed highly desirable in efficiency terms, even though the principal beneficiaries may not necessarily be the ones who bear the burden of the costs arising from the use. If this is the case, then this particular wetland use may be efficient but it may also have significant negative distributional consequences. It is therefore often important that many proposed wetland investments or management policies are assessed not only in terms of their efficiency but also their distributional implications.

The present study conducted shows that the deterioration of water quality in the Pallikaranai Marsh was the major issue raised by the respondents during the process of socio-economic survey followed by other problems in the Marsh. Due to the water deterioration in the marsh, in surrounding areas, the groundwater quality is affected.

Initiatives to Be Taken Up Immediately

- Handover the Pallikaranai Marshland to the Forests department for protection and conservation of the Marsh.
- **Ban dumping of waste and discharging sewage or industrial effluents into the Pallikaranai Marsh.** The dump yard in Perungudi should be closed and dumping of MSWs should be in the outskirts away from human habitants. The smoke which is generated on burning the garbage in the Perungudi dump yard is slow poisoning the people who are living around the dump yard and also people who pass by the dump yard in Pallikaranai Marsh.
- **Solve the issue of encroachments:** Preventive measures can be taken to include demarcation of the outer boundary of the wetland, control unauthorized human entry, and unauthorized fishing inside the wetland area.
- **Cleaning up the channels connecting the wetland** with its tributaries and distributaries to be taken on war footing to remove the impediments in water flow. The restored channels have to be maintained properly to avoid any blockage that causes undue flooding of catchments during monsoon. Unauthorized activities such as dredging and filling should be prevented.
- **Removal of overgrown aquatic weeds, especially *Eichhornia crassipes*, from the wetland** to help sustain the vegetation structure, water quality including salinity, habitat quality, and diversity, etc., of the system.
- **Green belts/tree planting** is suggested along the trails/path made along the boundary. The species should be selected based on their dust and sound-absorbing capacity and water tolerance.
- **Awareness and involvement of stakeholders** with the help of departments, institutions, universities, colleges, NGOs, etc.

Long-Term Policy Initiatives for Wetlands in Tamil Nadu Specific to Pallikaranai Marsh

- **Formation of an Authority for Wetland Conservation and Management in Tamil Nadu** with the Chief Secretary as the Chairman, Member Secretary as Secretary, Environment, and Forests, Government of Tamil Nadu involving a member from the Union Ministry of Environment and Forests (MoEF&CC), Government of India, stakeholders, government departments, institutions, universities, colleges, schools, non-governmental organizations. The departments to be involved are the Department of Forests, Tamil Nadu Pollution Control Board, Department of Environment, Public Works Department, Chennai Corporation, Pallikaranai Town Panchayat, Institute for Water Resources, Metro Water, CMWSSB, Law Department, etc. It is expected that this Authority serves as a Single Window System where all the activities to be undertaken in the wetlands should be through this Authority, whether it involves line department works, restoration works, recreation works, and research works. All the funding for the management of the marsh should be routed through this Authority.

- It is proposed that this Authority can have different wings/ committees/ individuals to look into various aspects of wetland management, development, and most importantly conservation.

- The Authority should consist of governmental officials, scientists, NGOs, and stakeholders from various sectors for efficient implementation. This should be people-oriented.

- Enactment of an Act for the conservation of wetlands in Tamil Nadu similar to the 'The Kerala Conservation Of Paddy Land And Wetland (Amendment) Act', 2011. (*An Act to amend the Kerala Conservation of Paddy Land and Wetland Act, 2008*).

- Economic valuation studies should be conducted and the WTP by the stakeholders should be determined not only for the stakeholders who live in and around the marsh but for the Chennai city as some have direct benefits from the marsh and others have an indirect benefit from the marsh. A **Pallikaranai Wetland Conservation Fund** may be generated. As all the stakeholders who are in and around the marsh and those who are indirectly benefited from the wetland should be (and a majority would be more than willing to pay) able to pay for the conservation of the marsh. This is more of an awareness and commitment to save and conserve the marsh. In the present study, the stakeholders who are generally from a low, middle class, and poorer background are interviewed and the men were ready to pay Rs. 101.94 per year and the women were ready to pay Rs. 98.11 per year. Even though the amount received from the stakeholders may be meager, this will affirm their commitment and interest in the preservation of the wetland. This is an initiative of the first of its kind in South India. The other funds can be channelized in a more transparent and logical manner from the Government of India, State Government, and other sources.

- The dump yards should be scientifically disbanded and from the literature, it is found that the floral diversity was high in Perungudi dump yard and the dominant plant species were *Lycopersicon esculentum, Benincasa cerifera, Acalypha indica, Phyllanthes amarus, Cyperus rotundus, and Cynodon dactylon*. Bermuda grass (*Cynodon dactylon*) and African marigold (*Tagetes erecta*) were grown at Kodungaiyur dump yard. No toxic symptoms were observed in plants, which grew, and established well in the dump yard and can be suitable plants to grow in tropical climates. Hence, the Bermuda grass and marigold can be employed in the remediation of dump yards.

- Except for the Okkiyam Maduvu, no other channels exist for the marsh. Channels are necessary to maintain ecosystem health, prevent drying up, and regain the hydrological balance of the wetland. The channels, which existed in the past with Pallikaranai Marsh, need to be identified and restored.

- Re-establishing links among the separated portions of the wetland ensuring flood control of the region as well as protects the wetland from losing the characteristics and to ensure species movements.

- Fishing may be allowed in only a few scientifically selected parts of the wetland and should be regulated.
- A wetland with a gradient of depth or heterogeneous depth profile will increase habitat diversity and thereby attract more species. Hence certain areas should be necessarily maintained given depths suitable for various species groups and also to maintain a proper hydro-period in the marsh.
- A research and monitoring committee may be set up with a panel of experts/consultants from various sectors, involving the local communities.
- Data management and GIS of the wetland and the surrounding areas should be developed and updated consistently.
- Monitoring of pollutants (air, water, soil) and other threats may be done periodically by independent research organizations. A survey may be conducted to locate point and non-point sources of pollution. Monitoring biodiversity (floral and faunal components) and basic physio-chemical parameters should be conducted seasonally over years.
- Pallikaranai Wetland can be named as Pallikaranai **Wetland Park**-first of its kind in India-like the Hong Kong Wetland Park, Mai Po Wetland Park in Hong Kong, Xixi National Wetland Park in China, etc. The wetland park should have an interpretation center, bird-watching towers, and other requirements in tune with the wetland parks in the Asian countries. This will evolve employment generation for the people living in and around the wetland.

Although these approaches can provide useful general input, the pressing need is to find a way to involve local residents meaningfully at a detailed, action-specific level, and recognize the complex, multi-dimensional nature of the types of program initiatives under consideration for the conservation and management of Pallikaranai Marsh.

ANNEXURE I

LIST OF FLORAL SPECIES RECORDED IN PALLIKARANAI MARSH

Sl. No.		Sl. No.	
1	Abutilon indicum	32	Ipomea carnea
2	Acalypha indica	33	Jatropha gossypifilia
3	Achyranthes aspera	34	Lantana camara
4	Alternanthera sessilis	35	Lemna sp.
5	Amaranthus spinosus	36	Leucas aspera
6	Amaranthus viridis	37	Mukia leiosperma
7	Astracanthus longifolius	38	Nymphaea pubescens
8	Bacopa sp.	39	Ottelia alismoides
9	Boerhavia diffusa	40	Parssiflora foetida
10	Brachiaria sp.	41	Parthenium hysterophorus
11	Calotropis gigantean	42	Phyla nodiflora
12	Cardiospermum halicacabum	43	Phyllanthus amarus
13	Cassia occidentals	44	Phyllanthus reticulotes
14	Cleome viscose	45	Physalis minima
15	Coccinia grantis	46	Pistia stratiotes
16	Crotilaria pallida	47	Prosophis juliflora
17	Croton vonplandianus	48	Ricinus communis
18	Cynodon dactylon	49	Ruellia tuberose
19	Cyprus rotundus	50	Sesuvium portulacastrum
20	Cyprus sp.	51	Sida sp.
21	Datura metel	52	Sphaeranthus indicus
22	Dolichos sp.	53	Stachytarpheta sp.
23	Echinochloa sp.	54	Trianthema portulacastrum
24	Eclipta prostrata	55	Tridax procumbens
25	Eichhornia crassipes	56	Turnera ulmifolia

Sl. No.		Sl. No.	
26	Evolvus alsinoides	57	Tylophora indica
27	Gomphrena celesioides	58	Typha anguistata
28	Heliotropium curassavicum	59	Utricularia stellaris
29	Heliotropium indicum	60	Wattakaka volubilis
30	Hydrilla verticillata	61	Xanthium indicum
31	Hygrophylla aurculata		

Source: Management Plan for the Eco-restoration of Pallikaranai Reserve Forest-Sálim Ali Centre for Ornithology and Natural History, Coimbatore, 2007.

ANNEXURE II

LIST OF FAUNAL SPECIES RECORDED IN PALLIKARANAI MARSH

Bird Species		
SI. No.	Common Name	Scientific Name
1	Little grebe	Tachybaptus ruficollis
2	Little cormorant	Phalacrocorax niger
3	Large cormorant	Phalacrocorax carbo
4	Spot-billed duck	Anas poecilorhyncha
5	Gray heron	Ardea cineria
6	Purple heron	Ardea purpurea
7	Cattle egret	Bubulcus ibis
8	Large egret	Casmerodius albus
9	Small egret	Mesophoyx intermedia
10	Little egret	Egretta garzetta
11	Pond heron	Ardeola grayii
12	Night heron	Nicticorax nicticorax
13	Black bittern	Ixobrychus flavicollis
14	Cinnamon bittern	Ixobrychus cinnamomeus
15	Yellow bittern	Ixobrychus chinensis
16	Spot-billed pelican	Pelecanus philippensis
17	Open-billed stork	Anastomus oscitans
18	Wooly-necked stork	Ciconia episcopus
19	Glossy ibis	Plegadis falcinellus
20	Black-headed ibis	Threskiornis melanocephalus
21	Pariah kite	Milvus migrans
22	Black-winged kite	Elanus caeruleus
23	Brahminy Kite	Haliastur Indus
24	Pale harrier	Circus macrourus
25	Pied harrier	Circus melanoleucos
26	Marsh harrier	Circus aeruginosus

Bird Species		
Sl. No.	**Common Name**	**Scientific Name**
27	Shikra	Accipiter badius
28	Kestral	Falco tannunculus
29	Indian moorhen	Gallinula chloropus
30	Purple moorhen	Porphyrio porphyrio
31	Coot	Fulica atra
32	Stone curlew	Burhinus oedicnemus
33	Great thick-knee	Burhinus recurvirostris
34	Red-necked phalarope	Phalaropus lobatus
35	Pheasant-tailed Jacana	Hydrophasianus chirurgus
36	Red-wattled lapwing	Vanellus indicus
37	Yelow-wattled lapwing	Vanellus malabaricus
38	Black-winged stilt	Himantopus himantopus
40	Marsh sandpiper	Tringa stagnatilis
41	Stint	Calidris sp.
42	Oriental pranticole	Glareola maldivarum
43	Snipe	Gallinago sp.
44	Black-tailed godwit	Limosa limosa
45	Whiskered tern	Chlidonias hybridus
46	White-winged black tern	Chlidonias leucopterus
47	Gull-billed tern	Gelochelidon nilotica
48	Blue-rock pigeon	Colomba livia
49	Spotted dove	Sterptopilia chinensis
50	Rose-ringed parakeet	Psittacula krameri
51	Asian koel	Eudynamys scolopacea
52	Hawk cuckoo	Cuculus varius
53	Pied-crested cuckoo	Oxylophus jacobinus
54	Spotted owlet	Athene brama
55	Barn owl	Tyto alba
56	Small-blue kingfisher	Alcedo atthis
57	White-breasted kingfisher	Halcyon smyrnensis
58	Pied kingfisher	Ceryle rudis
59	Indian roller	Coricias bengalensis
60	Blue-tailed bee-eater	Merops philippinus
61	Small-green bee-eater	Merops orientalis
62	Hoopoe	Upupa epops
63	House swift	Apus affinis
64	Palm swift	Cypsiurus batasiensis

Bird Species		
Sl. No.	**Common Name**	**Scientific Name**
65	Golden-backed woodpecker	Dinopium bengalensis
66	Barn swallow	Hirundo rustica
67	Wire-tailed swallow	Hirundo smithii
68	Ashy-crowned finch lark	Erimopterix grisea
69	Syke's-crested lark	Galerida deva
70	Oriental skylark	Alauda gulgula
71	Eurasian skylark	Alauda arvensis
72	Singing lark	Mirafra cantillans
73	Black-crowned finchlark	Eremopterix nigriceps
74	Common myna	Acridotheres tristis
75	Brahminy starling	Sturnus pagodarum
76	Asian-pied starling	Sturnus contra
77	House crow	Corvus splendens
78	Jungle crow	Corvus macrorhynchus
79	Indian treepie	Dendrocitta vagabunda
80	Red-vented bulbul	Pycnonotus cafer
81	Red-whiskered bulbul	Pycnonotus jocosus
82	Yellow-billed babbler	Turdoides affinis
83	Tailor bird	Orhtotomus sutorius
84	Ashy prinia	Prinia socialis
85	Plain prinia	Prinia inornata
86	Blyth's reed warbler	Acrocephalus dumetorum
87	Great reed warbler	Acrocephalus stentoreus
88	Streaked fantail warbler	Cisticola juncidis
89	Pied bush chat	Saxicola caprata
90	Magpie robin	Copsychus saularis
91	Orange-headed thrush	Zoothera citrine
92	Yellow wagtail	Motacilla flava
93	Large-pied wagtail	Motacilla maderaspatensis
94	Paddyfield pipit	Anthus novaeseelandiae
95	Richard's pipit	Anthus richardi
96	House sparrow	Passer domesticus
97	Streaked weaver bird	Ploceus manyar
98	Black-headed munia	Lonchura malacca
99	Black drongo	Dicrurus adsimilis
100	Ashy swallow-shrike	Artamus fuscus
101	Gray shrike	Lanius excubitor

Bird Species		
Sl. No.	**Common Name**	**Scientific Name**
102	Golden oriole	Oriolus oriolus
103	Loten's sunbird	Nectarinia lotenia
104	Gray francolin	Francolinus pondicerianus
105	White-breasted waterhen	Amaurornis phoenicurus
106	Water cock	Gallicrex cinerea
107	Painted snipe	Rostratula benghalensis
108	Little ringed plover	Chadrius dubius
109	Gray plover	Pluvialis squatarola
110	Indian river tern	Sterna aurantia
111	Indian roller	Coracias benghalensis
112	Zitting cisticola	Cisticola juncidis

Reptiles		
Sl. No.	**Common name**	**Scientific name**
1	Garden lizard	Calotes versicolor
2	Fan-throated lizard	Sitana ponticeriana
3	Common skink	Mabuya carinata
4	Garden skink	Lygosoma punctata
5	White-spotted garden skink	Yigosoma albopunctata
6	Indian monitor lizard	Varanus bhengalensis
7	Spotted gecko	Hemidactylus brooki
8	Termite-hill gecko	Hemidactylus triedrus
9	House gecko	Hemidactylus frenatus
10	Bark gecko	Hemidactylus leschenaultia
11	Blind snake	Rhamphotyphlops braminus
12	Striped keel back	Amphiesma stolata
13	Olive keel back	Atretium schistosum
14	Checkered keel back	Xeenochrophis piscator
15	Rat snake	Ptyas mucosus
16	Green vine snake	Ahaetulla nasutus
17	Cobra	Naja naja
18	Krait	Bungarus caeruleus
19	Russell's viper	Vipera russelli
20	Pond turtle	Melanichelys trijuga
21	Falpshel	Lissemys punctata

Amphibians		
Sl. No.	**Common name**	**Scientific name**
1	Indian pond frog	Euphlyctis hexadactylus
2	Skipper	Euphlyctis cynophlyctis
3	Burrowing frog	Tomopterna rolandae
4	Jerdon's bull frog	Hoplobathrachus crassus
5	Paddy Field frog	Limnonectes limnocharis
6	Painted frog	Kaloula taprobanica
7	Marbled frog	Ramanella variegata
8	Indian Toad	Bufo melanostictus
9	Common tree frog	Polypedates maculatus

Fishes		
Sl. No.	**Common name**	**Scientific name**
1	Long-fin eel	Anguilla benghalensis
2	Short-fin eel	Anguilla bicolor
3	Anchovy	Stolephorus sp.
4	Baril	Barilius bendelisis
5	Glass barb	Esomus danricus
6	Carplet	Amblyphryngodon microlepis
7	Black-line rasbora	Rasbora daniconius
8	Razor belly	Salmostoma clupeoides
9	Silver razor belly	Salmostoma acinaces
10	One-spot barb	Puntius filamentosus
11	Scarlet-banded barb	Puntius amphi
12	Spot-fin barb	Puntius sophore
13	Ticto barb	Puntius ticto
14	Peninsular olive barb	Barbodes sarana
15	Swamp barb	Puntius chola
16	Long-snouted barb	Puntius dorsalis
17	Fringe-lipped peninsular carp	Labeo fimbriatus
18	Loach	Lepidocephalus thermalis
19	Gangetic mystus	Mystus cavasius
20	Long-whiskered catfish	Mystus gulio
21	Striped dwarf catfish	Mystius gulio
22	River catfish	Aorichthys aor
23	Giant river catfish	Aorichthys seenghala
24	Stinging catfish	Heteropneustes fossilis
25	Indian potassi	Pseudeutropius atherinoides

Fishes		
Sl. No.	Common name	Scientific name
26	Magur	Clarias batrachusq
27	Panchax	Aplochelius parvus
28	Half beak	Hyporahamphus limbatus
29	Rice fish	Oryzias melastigma
30	Mosquito fish	Gambusia affinis
31	Spotted snake head	Channa punctatus
32	Striped snake head	Channa striatus
33	Asiatic snake head	Channa orientalis
34	Giant snake head	Channa marulius
35	Orange chromide	Etroplus maculates
36	Green chromide	Etroplus suratensis
37	Tilapia	Oreochromis mossambicus
38	Glass fish	Ambassis commersonii
39	Tank goby	Glossogobius giurus
40	Climbing perch	Anabas testudineus
41	Dwarf gourami	Colisa lalia
42	Spike tailed paradise fish	Macropodus cupanus
43	One stripe spiny eel	Macrognathus aral
44	Striped spiny eel	Macrognathus pancalus
45	Mullet	Liza parsia
46	Tire tracked spiny eel	Mastacembelus armatus

Butterflies		
Sl. No.	Common name	Scientific name
1	Lime butterfly	Papilio demoleus
2	Mottled emigrant	Catopsilia pyranthe
3	Common crow	Euploea core
4	Plain tiger	Danaus chrysippus
5	Glassy tiger	Parantica aglaea
6	Peacock pansy	Junonia almanac
7	Tawny coster	Acraea violae

Crustaceans		
Sl. No.	**Common name**	**Scientific name**
1	Prawn	Paliemon sp.
2	Fresh water prawn	Macrobrachium rosenburgii
3	Pond crab	Paratelphusa sp.
4	Mud crab	Scylla cerrata
5	Fresh water shrimp	

Molluscs		
Sl. No.	**Common name**	**Scientific name**
1	Windowpane oyster	Placenta placenta
2	Arc shell	Arca spp.
3	Oyster	Crassostrea spp.
4	Apple snail	Pyla virens
5	Fresh water mussel	Lamellidens marginalis
6	Fresh water snail	Plidomus sp.
7	Fresh water snail	Thiara sp.
8	Fresh water snail	Lymnaea sp.
9	Ram's horn snail	Indoplanorbis exustus

Mammals		
SI No.	**Common name**	**Scientific name**
1	Spotted deer	Axis axis
2	Bonnet macaque	Macaca radiata
3	Indian pipistrelle	Pipistrellus coromandra
4	Leaf-nosed bat	Hipposideros sp.
5	Three-striped palm squirrel	Funambulus palmarum
6	Bandicoot	Badicota bengalensis
7	House rat	Rattus rattus
8	Mice	Mus sp.
9	Jackal	Cannis aureus
10	Mongoose	Herpestes edwarsii

Source: Management Plan for the Eco-restoration of Pallikaranai Reserve Forest- Sálim Ali Centre for Ornithology and Natural History, Coimbatore- 2007

ANNEXURE III

QUESTIONNAIRE SCHEDULE FOR HOUSEHOLD WILLINGNESS TO PAY FOR CONSERVATION AND MANAGEMENT OF PALLIKARNAI MARSH

Date: _______________   Interview starting time: _______________

Household No : _______________   **Ward No:** _______________

Hamlet : _______________

Address: House no : _______________

Street : _______________

I. General Information about the Respondent/Household

1. Sex of the Respondent: Male/Female
2. Age of the Respondent: _______________
3. Respondent's Name: _______________
4. Respondent's Education: _______________
5. Whether head of the household? yes/no
6. Family Status: nuclear/joint family
7. No. of years living in this area: _______________
8. No of household members living for the last six months: (including the respondent)

Members	Age	Sex	Education	Relation to Respondent
No.1				
No.2				
No.3				

Members	Age	Sex	Education	Relation to Respondent
No.4				
No.5				
No.6				
Others (Specify)				

II. Environment-Related Problems

According to you which of the following problems in your area is most important for you?

1. Sanitation
2. Water Supply
3. Drainage
4. Garbage
   Any other ________________.

A. Waste Water Usage:

1. Is your household connected with the drainage system? yes/no.
2. If no, what happens to:
   Kitchen water?
   Bathroom water?
   Washing water?

   ____

3. If yes, is all the wastewater going to the drainage system? yes/no.
4. If no, where does the remaining water go?

   ____________________.

5. Is drainage creating any problem? yes/no.
6. If yes, what kind of the problem?
   (i) —————————————————————-
   (ii) —————————————————————-
   (iii) ————————————————————
7. Do you spend anything for removing the wastewater? yes/no.
8. If yes, how much per month? Rs. __________

B. Water and Health

1. Are you aware of any water borne diseases? yes/no.
2. If yes, what are diseases?
   (i.) _____________________
   (ii.) _____________________
   (iii.) _______________________
3. Do you boil water before using for drinking purpose? yes/no.
4. Are you aware of any of the following illnesses?
   (i.) Diarrhea
   (ii.) Jaundice
   (iii.) Typhoid
   (iv.) Malaria

III. Sources of Water Supply

1. **Different Sources of Water Supply for the Household**
   (a) Public Tap/Ground Level Reservoir (GLR) yes/no
        (if yes, go to section III. a)
   (b) Individual connection   yes/no
        (if yes, go to section III. b)
   (c) Hand pumps   yes/no
        (if yes, go to section III. c)
   (d) Own well   yes/no
        (if yes go, to section III. d)
   (e) Private agricultural borewells   yes/no
        (if yes go, to section III. e)
2. **Do you have storage facility in your house? yes/no.**
3. **if yes,**
   No. of Kodams_______(Total Capacity in liters:__________).
   No. of Buckets_______(Total Capacity in liters:__________).
   No. of Cement tanks____(Total Capacity in liters: _________).
   No. of Barrels_______(Total Capacity in liters:__________).
   Any other (specify) _______(Total Capacity in liters:_________).

4. **Is the existing storage facility in your household adequate for storing water at present?** yes/no.
5. **If yes, do you think you can store additional quantity of water with the existing storage facility?** yes/no.
6. **If no to Question nos. 7 and 8, will you be able to expand the capacity of the storage facility if additional water is available to you?** yes/no.

A. For Households Collecting Water from Public Tap:

1. **How far is the nearest public tap from your house?**
    No. of feet: _________________ One way travel time: _____________
2. **How many households collect water from this tap, including your household?**
3. **How many persons are involved in collecting water in your household?**
    No. of persons: _____________
4. **How many trips do you make per day per head?**
    No. of trips: ___________________
5. **Is there any restriction in collecting water from the stand post?**

	At present	Past
In terms of quantity	Yes/no.	Yes/no.
In terms of no. of person.	Yes/no.	yes/no.

6. **What kind of the method of collection of water is followed by you and your neighboring households from this particular public tap?**
    (a.) Based on the number of families in a household
    (b.) Based on the household (irrespective of the size and no. of families in a household)
    (c.) Based on the quantity of water (i. e. each household can collect only a specified amount)
7. **In a week, how many days do you get water from the public tap?**
    No. of Days: At present__________   Past _________
8. **How many hours do you get water?**
    No. of Days: At present__________   Past _________

9. **When does the water come?**
   Morning /Afternoon/Evening/Night/Anytime.
10. **What is the quantity of water that you can collect per week on an average?**
    No. of Kodams: At present ____________ Past __________
11. **How much time do you spent in collecting water per head per time?**
    Travel time per head: At present ____________Past __________
    Waiting time per head: At present ____________Past __________
    No. of hours per head: At present ____________Past __________
    Total hours: **At present ____________Past __________**
12. **How do you perceive the quality of water in terms of:**
    (a.) Color   :   very good/good/bad.
    (b.) Taste   :   very good/good/bad.
    (c.) Dust   :   very good/good/bad.
    (d.) Ability to boil things :   very good/good/bad.
    (e.) Softness   :   very good/good/bad.
13. **What purposes do you use this water for and what is the quantity used per day cin terms of kodam?**
    Drinking ________; Cooking______; Washing __________;
    Bathing ________; Cleaning ________; Cattle ______;
    Others ________.
14. **Do you experience any of the following problems regarding water supply from public tap?**
    (i.) Quantity is not adequate
    (ii.) Timing is not convenient
    (iii.) Distance is high
    (iv.) Frequency of the supply is not convenient

B. For Households with Individual Connection

1. **When did you get the individual connection?** ____________
2. **Did you pay any deposit?**
3. **If yes, how much? Rs.** __________
4. **What were the other total expenses? Rs.** __________

5. **Is the tap in this house working?** yes/no.
6. **If no, why is it not working?**
   - Technical Problem
   - Water cut for not paying the bill
   - Any other (specify) _______________________
7. **In a week, how many days do you get water from your tap?**
   No. of days: At present __________   Past __________
8. **How many hours per day do you get water?**
   Hours: At present __________   Past __________
9. **When does the water come?**
   Morning/Afternoon/Evening/Night/Anytime
10. **What is the quantity of water that you collect per week on an average?**
    No. of Kodams: At present __________   Past __________
11. **How much time do you spend collecting water per supply?**
    No. of hours per supply: At persent ______   Past __________
12. **How do you perceive the quality of water from the stand post in terms of:**
    (a.) Color   :   very good/good/bad.
    (b.) Taste   :   very good/good/bad.
    (c.) Dust   :   very good/good/bad.
    (d.) Ability to boil things :   very good/good/bad.

C. For Households Collecting Water from Hand pumps:

1. **How far is the hand pipe from which you collect water from your house?**
   No. of yards: ____________   One way travel time: __________
2. **How many persons are involved in fetching water from hand pipe?**
3. **How many trips do you/they make per day per head?**
   No. of trips: ____________
4. **What is the quantity of water that you collect per week on an average?**
   No. of Kodams: At present __________   Past __________

5. **How much time do you spent in collecting water per head per time?**

		At present	Past
Travel time per head	:	_________	_________
Waiting time per head	:	_________	_________
No. of hours per head	:	_________	_________
Total hours	:	_________	_________

6. **How do you perceive the quality of water from the hand pipe in terms of:**
   (a.) Color   :   very good/good/bad.
   (b.) Taste   :   very good/good/bad.
   (c.) Dust   :   very good/good/bad.
   (d.) Ability to boil things :   very good/good/bad.
   (e.) Softness   :   very good/good/bad.
   (f.) Washing clothes   :   very good/good/bad.

7. **Do you experience any of the following problems regarding water supply from the hand pump?**
   (i.) Quantity is not adequate
   (ii.) Timing is not convenient
   (iii.) Distance is high
   (iv.) Frequency of the supply is not convenient

8. **What purposes do you use this water for and what is the quantity used per day?**
   Drinking _______; Cooking _________; Washing __________;
   Bathing ______; Cleaning _________; Cattle ________;
   Others ________

D. For Households Collecting Water from Private Agricultural Borewells

1. **How far is the agricultural borewell from your house?**
   No. of yards: ____________One way travel time: ___________

2. **How many persons are involved in fetching water from the agricultural borewell?**
   No. of persons _____________

3. **How many trip as do you/they make per day per head?**
    No. of trips: ___________   Total trips __________

4. **What is the quantity of water that you collect per week on an average?**
    No. of Kodams: At present _______   Past __________

5. **How much time do you spent in collecting water per head per time?**
    Travel time per head   : ____________
    Waiting time per head   : ____________
    No. of hours per head   : ____________
    Total hours   : ____________

5a. **Have you employed anybody to fetch water from the agricultural borewell?**
    yes/no.

E. For Households Having their Own Borewells

1. **When did you install the borewell?** _____________

2. **How much did it cost you?**
    Motor   Rs. ___________
    Pipes   Rs. ___________
    Installing Charge   Rs. ___________

3. **What is the monthly electricity bill toward running the electric motor?**
    Rs. ___________

4. **How much of water do you collect per day on an average?**
    No. of Kodams: At present _______   Past __________

5. **What purposes do you use this water for and what is the quantity used per days?**
    Drinking ________; Cooking _________; Washing _______;
    Bathing ________; Cleaning _______; Cattle ______;
    Others ________

6. **How do you perceive the quality of water from your well in terms of:**

    (a.) Color   :   very good/good/bad.
    (b.) Taste   :   very good/good/bad.
    (c.) Dust   :   very good/good/bad.
    (d.) Ability to boil things   :   very good/good/bad.
    (e.) Softness   :   very good/good/bad.
    (f.) Washing Clothes   :   very good/good/bad.

6a. **What purpose do you use this water for and what is the quantity use per day?**

    Drinking ________; Cooking _________; Washing _______;
    Bathing ________;
    Cleaning _________; Cattle __________; Others __________

IV. Other General Aspects:

1. **Are there any other sources of water supply?** yes/no.

2. **If yes, what are the alternative sources available?**

    ____

    ____

3. **Why do you choose these sources?**

    ____

4. **How do you manage your water requirement during special occasions, if any?**

    ____

5. **Do you have anything to say about the water supply situation in your area?**

    ____

    ____

Total quantity of water per week from all sources (average)
(In terms of Kodams with 12 liters capacity)

Public Taps/	Individual Connections	Hand pumps	Own wells	Agril. Borewells	Others
Quantity					

Quantity of water used for all purposes per month (average)
(In terms of Kodams with 12 liters capacity)

Drinking	Cooking	Bathing	Washing	Cattle	Others	Total
Quantity						

V. Contingent Valuation Scenarios:

PERCEPTION ABOUT PALLIKARNAI MARSH, CHENNAI

1. **What are the important problems in Chennai?**

Problem	Very important	Important	Not important	Don't know
Unemployment				
Crime				
Environmental pollution				
Education				
Corruption				

2. **Which is the important Environmental problem in Chennai, in your perception?**

Environmental Problems	Very important	Important	Not important	Don't know
Deforestation Urban Waste/ Solid waste pollution Noise pollution Vehicular pollution Industrial pollution Air pollution				
Poor drinking water supply				
Noise pollution				
Pollution in Water bodies				

3. **Are you living in Chennai?** (Yes / No)
4. **If yes, how many years?** (Yes / No)
5. **Are you aware that the Pallikaranai Marsh in Alandur Municipality is degrading?**
6. **Do you know the importance of the marsh?**
7. **Please rank the following statement:**
   "Important wetlands like the Pallikaranai Marsh require special conservation measures."
   Strongly agree
   Agree
   Neutral
   Disagree
   Strongly disagree
8. **You may be aware that the Wetland provides a number of services to the citizens of this city. A few of them are listed below. Kindly rank them according to their importance in your opinion.**
   1 - most important
   2 - very important
   3 - important
   4 - somewhat important
   5 - least important
   Services Ranking
   Drinking Water
   Stability of microclimate
   Employment to fishermen
   Recreation and tourism (Bird watching and walking path)
9. **How often do you go to the Pallikaranai Marsh**
   Every week
   Once in a fortnight
   Once in a month
   Once in two - six months
   Once in seven - twelve months

10. **To what extent is the Pallikaranai Marsh polluted in your opinion?**
    a) Marginally
    b) Moderately
    c) Highly
    d) Not at all

11. **How would you rank the various threats to the Pallikaranai Marsh in order of importance?**
    1 - most important
    2 - very important
    3 - important
    4 - somewhat important
    5 - least important
    Problem Ranking
    a. Siltation
    b. Solid waste pollutants /Municipal Dumping of Wastes
    c. Sewage
    d. Washermen
    f. Encroachment
    g. Increasing population
    h. Weeds and eutrophication
    m. Others, please specify

12. **Suppose that the Pallikaranai Marsh was continuing to disappear tomorrow and a person like you had a chance to save this particular area. Are you willing to pay to save this marsh for your future generations?**

13. **How do you rate the Pallikaranai Marsh water?**
    (a) good
    (b) bad
    (c) worst

14. **While rating the water in terms of quality, which of the following aspects did you take into account?**
    (a.) Taste ();
    (b) Ability to cooking food ();
    (c) Softness to take bath ();

(d) Ability to preserve remaining food ();

(e) Any other ___________.

Scenario –Formation of a committee for the Conservation of the Pallikarnai Marsh and Pallikaranai Wetland Conservation Fund.

To save the Pallikaranai Marsh a committee can be formed consisting of Forest Department, Tourism Department, and Municipal Corporation. This committee can implement the projects for sustainable use of the Pallikaranai Marsh.

1. Stop dumping of garbage and discharge of sewerage in the marsh. I understand several steps have already been taken in this direction. It requires more vigorous implementation.
2. Stop sanctioning any more reclamation and construction on reclaimed land in and around the marsh.
3. Acquire all the unused land, which are part of the original marsh. Clear the remaining part of the marsh and the acquired lands of all encroachments.
4. Clear/remove all the garbage form the marsh.
5. Dredge out the silt completely from the marsh and deepen the marsh substantially.
6. Fill up to about 100 feet width on the sides of the existing roads in the marsh such as the Thoraipakkam-Pallavaram road, Sholinganallur -Medavakkam road etc. with good soil, and develop gardens in these patches with proper fencing on the roadside to prevent grazing.
7. Trees can be planted on the sides of the lake too for the birds to nest like in the Vedanthangal Lake. The number of birds visiting the marsh will increase substantially making it a virtual bird sanctuary.
8. With the water level rising substantially in the marsh – can even be called a lake – pleasure boating can be introduced.
9. Swimming pools can be built, an aquarium established, and many water sporting facilities can be developed.

With the implementation of the above steps, pollution will be minimized substantially. The vegetation will absorb the traces of pollution left.

Rainwater harvesting and groundwater recharge will be the major benefit along with reducing the salinity in the groundwater. The marsh can be turned in to a place of tourist attraction and all the subsequent maintenance of the garden and the lake can be funded by gate collection and the boating collection itself. Off course, we will have to ensure that the visitors – tourists – themselves do not pollute the lake again. The restoration of the lake and raising the garden can be done with community involvement. We have already got a few good examples of such campaigns yielding excellent results. The water quality of the marsh will improve.

VI. SOCIO-ECONOMIC STATUS

1. **Is your house owned/rented?**
2. **Type of the house:**
   i.) Storeyed
   ii.) Tiled
   iii.) Roofed
   iv.) Any other (specify)
3. **If rented, how much rent do you pay per month?** Amount Rs. ___________
3a. **If owned, how much rent it would fetch if rented?** Amount Rs. ___________
4. **Does your household have electricity?** yes/no.
5. **If yes, what is the average electricity bill per month?**
   Amount Rs. ___________
6. **What is the average monthly expenditure of regular consumption items?** (Including house rent, electricity & water bill exchange durable items.)
   Rs. ___________
7. **Income of the Individual respondent (per month)(both men and women respondents)**

Below 500	501-1000	1001-2000	2001-3500	3501-5000	5001-7500	7501-10000	Above 10000

8. **Do you have agricultural land?** yes/no.

9. **If yes, what did you cultivate this year?**

    i.) _______________________________________

    ii) _______________________________________

    iii) ______________________________________

10. **What is the average annual net farm income?**

    Rs. ______ ______ per annum.

11. **Does your household own any of the following items?**

    Items   Number

    ———————————————————————————————————-

    Radio

    Cooker

    Fan

    Bicycle

    TV

    Automobile

    No. of Cows

    No. of Bullocks

    No. of Buffaloes

    No. of Goats

    No. of Sheep

    Any other (specify)

12. **Occupation:**

    How many adults have employment? _____________

Persons	Sex M/F or Men and Women	Occupation	Monthly Income	Age	Edun.
1.					
2.					
3.					
4.					
Total					

13. **Do you get regular income from any other sources?** yes/no.

14. **If yes, how much per month?** Rs. _____________ per month.

15. **Annual income from all sources:**
    Amount Rs. _________________

16. **Income range of the Household per month:**

Below 500	501-1001	1001-2000	2001-3500	3501-5000	5001-7500	7501-10000	Above 10000

Interview ending time _________________
Duration of Interview _________________

ANNEXURE IV

SOCIO-ECONOMIC CHARACTERISTICS OF RESPONDENTS

▼ **Table 6.4.1.7:** Occupation of Male Respondents

Occupation of male respondents	Number of respondents	Percentage
No occupation	-	0
Government job	8	12
Private job	19	28
Self-employed	40	60
GRAND TOTAL	**67**	**100**

▼ **Table 6.4.1.8:** Occupation of Female Respondents

Occupation of female respondents	Number of respondents	Percentage
No occupation	42	25
Government job	4	2
Private job	20	12
Self-employed	100	61
GRAND TOTAL	**166**	**100**

▼ **Table 6.4.1.9:** Number of Members Employed in the Respondents Household

Number of members employed in the respondents household	Number of respondents	Percentage
1	121	52
2	95	41
3	11	5
4	6	2
Total	**233**	**100**

▼ **Table 6.4.1.10:**   Water Source for the Respondents

Water source	Number of respondents	Percentage
No source	2	1
Public tap	211	90
Individual connection	16	7
Hand pumps	2	1
Own well	2	1
Grand total	233	100

▼ **Table 6.4.1.11.1:**   Household Items Owned By Respondents

Entertainment	Number of respondents	Percentage
Radio	30	13
Television	83	36
Radio and Television	120	51
Total	233	100

▼ **Table 6.4.1.11.2:**   Household Items Owned By Respondents

House wares	Number of respondents	Percentage
None	0	0
Cooker	1	0
Fan	32	14
Cooker & Fan	200	86
Total	233	100

▼ **Table 6.4.1.12:**   Vehicles Owned By Respondents

Vehicles owned	Number of respondents	Percentage
None	86	37
Motorcycle	134	57
Auto-rickshaw	10	4
Motorcycle& Auto-rickshaw	3	2
Total	233	100

REFERENCES

© Can Stock Photo - csp14976258

APHA (1998), Standard Methods for the Examination of Water and Waste water, *American Public Health Association*, Washington, DC, USA.

Arrow, K, R. Solow, P. R. Portney, E. E. Leamer, R. Radner and Schuman (1993), "Report of the NOAA Panel on Contingent Valuation", Report to the General Counsel of the US National Oceanic and Atmospheric Administration, *Resources for the Future*, Washington, D.C.

Azeez, P. A, S. Bhupathy, J. Ranjini, R. Dhanya, P. P. Nikhil Raj (2007), "Management Plan for the Eco-restoration of Pallikaranai Reserve Forest", *Sálim Ali Centre for Ornithology and Natural History*, Coimbatore.

Bandyopadhyay, S, K. Narayanan and A. Ramanathan (2005), "Social perceptions and valuation of urban wetlands of Kolkata region" Fourth Biennial Conference of Indian Society for ecological economics (INSEE), pp. 1-12.

Barbier, E. B, M. Acreman and D. Knowler (1997), "Economic Valuation of Wetlands: A Guide for Policy Makers and Planners", Gland, Switzerland, *Ramsar Convention Bureau.*

Barbier, E. B (1989), "The Economic Value of Ecosystems:1 – Tropical Wetlands", LEEC Gatekeeper Series 89-02, *London Environmental Economics Centre,* London.

Bateman, I. J, I. H. Langford, K. G. Willis, R. K. Turner and G. D. Garrod (1993), "The Impacts of Changing Willingness to Pay Question Format in Contingent Valuation Studies: An Analysis of Open-ended, Iterative Bidding and Dichotomous Choice Formats", CSERGE Working Paper, School of Environmental Sciences, University of East Anglia, Norwich.

Binilkumar, A. S and A. Ramanathan (2009), "Valuing Stakeholder preferences on Improved Conservation and Management of Kol Wetland: A Contingent Valuation Study", Presented *at 11th Annual BIOECON Conference on Economic Instruments to Enhance the Conservation and Sustainable Use of Biodiversity* held on 21 - 22 September, 2009 at Centro Culturale Don Orione Artigianelli - Venice, Italy.

Briscoe, J, P. F. de Castro and C. Griffin (1990), "Toward equitable and sustainable rural water supplies: a contingent valuation study in Brazil", *World Bank Economic Reviews,* Vol. 4, No. 2, pp. 115-34.

Care Earth (2002), "Pallikaranai Marsh biodiversity assessment- First comprehensive report of the importance of the flood plain", Supported by the Tamil Nadu Pollution Control Board, Chennai and Care Earth Trust, Chennai.

Care Earth (2005), "Pallikaranai Marsh Evaluation", Supported by Tamil Nadu Pollution Control Board, Chennai and Care Earth Trust, Chennai.

Carson, R. T and D. Steinberg (1990), "Experimental design for discrete choice voter preference surveys", Proceeding of the Survey Methodology Section of the American Statistical Association. Washington, DC.

CCC and AR (Centre for Climate Change and Adaptation Research) Report (2011), "Identification of Pollution Source, Biodiversity Degradation and Adaptive Mechanism for Sustainable Management of Pallikaranai Marshland" CCC&AR, Anna University, Chennai.

CGWB (Central Ground Water Board) Report (2004), "Ground water scenario in Maharashtra- effect of water quality on human health", CGWB, GOI, New Delhi.

CGWB (Central Ground Water Board), Report (2010), "Report on hydrochemistry of landfill sites in Pallikaranai- Chennai: sub urban area, Tamil Nadu, South eastern coastal region, Chennai", Central Ground Water Board, Ministry of Water Resources, Government of India.

Central Pollution Control Board (CPCB) (2000), "Environmental standards for ambient air, automobiles, fuels, industries and noise, pollution control law series", Central Pollution Control Board, Ministry of Environment and Forests, New Delhi.

Central Public Health and Environmental Engineering Organisation (CPHEEO) (1999), "Manual on water supply and treatment", CPHEEO, Ministry of Urban Development, Government of India.

Chandramohan, B. P and Bharathi D (2009), "Role of Public Governance in the Conservation of Urban Wetland System: A Study of Pallikkaranai Marsh", *The Indian Society for Ecological Economics (INSEE)*: 5th Biennial Conference, Technical Session-III, pp. 1-22.

Chandrasekaran, Karthikeyan, Sureshkumar Devarajulu and Palanisami Kuppannan, (2009), "Farmers' Willingness to Pay for Irrigation Water: A Case of Tank Irrigation Systems in South India", *Water*, Vol. 1, pp 5-18.

Chenna, krishnan C, A. Stephen, T. Manju and R. Raveen (2008), "Water quality status of three vulnerable freshwater lakes of suburban Chennai, India", *Indian J. Environ and Eco plan*, Vol. 15, No. 3, pp 591 -596.

Coles, B and J. Coles, (1989), "Peopleof the Wetlands, Bogs, Bodies and Lake-Dwellers", *Thames and Hudson*, New York, pp. 709.

Community Environmental Monitoring (CEM) (2006)," Smoke Screen: Ambient air qualityin India", www. sipcotcudalore. com.

Corp Watch India (2002), "Trashing Water is Good Business For Water Companies", http://www. corpwatchindia. org / issues/PID.

Dams, Rivers and People (2004), South Asia Network on Dams, Rivers & People, Delhi, India, Vol. 2, Issue. No. 2, 3, 4.

Davis, T. J (ed.) (1993), "Towards the wise use of wetlands", Wise Use Project, *Ramsar Convention Bureau*, Gland, Switzerland.

Davies, Jon and Claridge Gordo (1993), "Wetland benefits:The potential for wetlands to support and maintain development", Published by: *Asian Wetland Bureau; International Waterfowl and Wetlands Research Bureau; Wetlands for the Americas.*

Deepa, R. S. and T. V. Ramachandra (1999), "Impact of Urbanisation in the interconnectivity of wetlands", National Symposium on Remote Sensing Applications for Natural Resources: Retrospective and perspective,(Jan 19-21,1999) organised by Indian Society of Remote Sensing, Bangalore.

Drescher Axel, Rüdiger Glaser, Constanze Pfeiffer, Jayshree Vencatesan, Elke Schliermann-Kraus, Stephanie Glaser, Marco Lechner, Paul Dostal (2007), "Risk assessment of extreme precipitation in the coastal areas of Chennai as an element of catastrophe prevention", Forum DKKV/CEDIM: Disaster Reduction in Climate Change, Karlsruhe University, Germany

Dugan, P. J (1990), "Wetland Conservation: a Review of Current Issues and Required Action" IUCN, Gland, Switzerland.

Durfor, C. N. and E. Becker (1964), "Public water supplies of the 100 largest cities in the United States", U. S Geological Survey Water Supply Paper, 1812, pp. 364-370 The Nalco Water Handbook. New York: *McGraw-Hill Book Co.*

Ellis, J. A (1980), "Convenient parameter for tracing leachate from sanitary landfills", *Water Res*, Vol. 14, pp. 1283-1287.

Ellison, JC (2009), "Wetlands of the Pacific Island Region" *Wetlands Ecology and Management*, Vol. 17, No. 3, pp. 169-206.

Erwin, Kevin. L (2009), "Wetlands and global climate change: the role of wetland restoration in a changing world", *Wetlands Ecol Management*, Vol. 17, pp. 71–84.

Esakku, S, Obuli P. Karthikeyan, Kurian Joseph, R. Nagendran, K. Palanivelu, K. P. M. N. Pathirana, A. K. Karunarathna and B. F. A. Basnayake (2007), "Seasonal Variations in Leachate Characteristics from Municipal Solid Waste Dumpsites in India and Srilanka", *Proceedings of the International Conference on Sustainable Solid Waste Management*, 5-7 September 2007, Chennai, India, pp. 341-347

Fletcher, G. D (1986), "Groundwater and wells", 2nd ed., *Johnson Division Publ.*, Sr. Paul Mimnesala, pp. 1089.

Freeman, A. M (1993), "The Measurement of Environmental and Resource Values", *Resources for the Future*, Washington DC. Gamble, J. S (1956), "Flora of the Presidency of Madras", Botanical Survey of India, Calcutta, Vol. II, pp. 942.

Glaser, S, R. Glaser, A. Drescher, C. Pfeiffer, E. Schliermann-Kraus, M. Lechner, J. Vencatesan (2008), "Geo-communication for risk assessment and catastrophe prevention of flood events in the coastal areas of Chennai", International Congress on Environmental Modelling and Software Integrating Sciences and Information Technology for Environmental Assessment and Decision Making, 4th Biennial Meeting, IEMSS, 2008.

Gopal, Brij (1996), "Overview of lakes and wetlands in India", in: Ando, M. (ed.) Conservation and Management of Lakes/Reservoirs in India, pp. 1-17, International Lake Environment Committee Foundation, Kusatsu, Shiga, Japan.

Hadker, Nandini, Sudhir Sharma, Ashish David and T. R. Muraleedharan (1997), "Willingness-to-pay for Borivli National Park: evidence from a Contingent Valuation", *Ecological Economics*, Vol. 21, pp. 105-122.

Hasan, I, Rajia. S (2009), "Comparative Study on the Water Quality Parameters in Two Rural and Urban Rivers Emphasizing on the

Pollution Level", *Global Journal of Environmental Research*, Vol. 3, pp. 218-222.

Hem, J. D (1985), "Study and interpretation of the chemical characteristics of natural water" (3rd edition): U. S Geological Survey Water-Supply Paper 2254, pp. 263.

Hooper, D. U, F. S. Chapin, J. J. Ewel, A. Hector, P. Inchausti, S. Lavorel, J. H. Lawton, D. M. Lodge, M. Loreau, S. Naeem, B. Schmid, H. Setälä, A. J. Symstad, J. Vandermeer and D. A. Wardle (2005), "Effects of biodiversity on ecosystem functioning: a consensus of current knowledge" *Ecological Monographs*. Vol. 5, No. 75, pp. 3–35.

Imandoust S. B and S. N. Gadam (2007), "Are people willing t o pay for river water quality, contingent valuation", *Int. J. Environ. Sci. Tech*, Vol. 4, No. 3, pp. 401-408.

IS 10500: 1991: Edition 2.1 (1993-01), Indian Standard Drinking Water -Specification (First Revision), BIS 2003, Bureau of Indian Standard, New Delhi.

IUCN (1990), "Directory of Wetlands of International Importance", *Ramsar Convention Bureau*, Gland Switzerland, pp. 796.

Jaganathan, R, K. Chelvaraajhan and S. Mahalingam (2010), "Geomatics Based Assessment on Land use Changes and its Impact over the Groundwater Conditions in a newly developing sub urban area –A Case of Southern Chennai", *International Journal of Geomatics and Geosciences*, Vol. 1, No. 3, pp. 271-281.

Jalali, Mohsen (2005), "Agriculture, Ecosystems and Environment", Volume. 110, Issue. 3–4, pp. 210–218.

Jameel, A and J.Sirajudeen (2006), "Risk assessment of physico-chemical contaminants in groundwater of Pettavaithalai area, Tiruchirappalli, Tamil Nadu". *India.Environ Monit Assess.*Vol. 123, No. 1-3, pp 299-312.

Jayakumar, S, Joon Heo, Il-Hong Seo and Hyoung Sig Cho (2009), "Rapid assessment of influential factors on Pallikaranai wetland of Tamil Nadu, India", *In Proceeding of Conference of The Korean Society for Geo Spatial Information System, April 24, 2009, Seoul, Korea*, pp. 329-331.

Jayaprakash, M, B. Urban P. M. Velmurugan, S. Srinivasalu (2010), "Accumulation of total trace metals due to rapid urbanization in microtidal zone of Pallikaranai Marsh, South of Chennai, India", *Environ Monit Assess*, Vol. 170, pp. 609–629.

Jinwal, A and Dixit. S (2008), "Pre-and Post Monsoon Variation in Physico Chemical Characteristics in Groundwater Quality of Bhopal "The City of Lakes" India", *Journal Exp. Sci*, Vol. 22, pp. 311-316.

Joint Committee Report (2003), "Threats to Pallikaranai wetland and need for its immediate remedial measures", Ministry of Environment and Forest, Government of India, New Delhi.

Karanth, K. R (1987), "Groundwater assessment, development and management" *Tata McGraw-Hill Publ. Co. Ltd*, pp. 720.

Karthikeyan, Obuli P, S. Murugesan, Kurian Joseph, Ligy Philip (2011), "Characterization of Particulate Matters and Volatile Organic Compounds in the Ambient Environment of Open Dump Sites", *Universal Journal of Environmental Research and Technology* Vol. 1, No. 2, pp. 140-150.

Kerry, Turner. R, C. J. M. Jeroen van den Bergh, Tore So derqvist, Aat Barendregt, Jan van der Straaten, Edward Maltby, Ekko-vanIerland (2000), "Ecological-economic analysis of wetlands: scientific integration for management and policy. Special Issue the Values of Wetlands: Landscape and Institutional Perspectives", *Ecological Economics* Vol. 35, pp 7–23.

Kumar, Anju A, S. Dipu and V. Sobha (2011), "Seasonal Variation of Heavy Metals in Cochin Estuary and Adjoining Periyar and Muvattupuzha Rivers, Kerala, India", *Global Journal of Environmental Research*, Vol. 5, No. 1, pp. 15-20.

Lee, S. M, K. D. Min, N. C. Woo, Y. J. Kim, C. H. Ahn (2003), "Statistical assessment of nitrate contamination in urban groundwater using GIS", *Environ Geology*, Vol. 44, pp. 210–221.

Lehr, J. H. and D. J. Pinkava (1980), "A catalogue of the flora of Arizona, Supplement I". *Journal of the Arizona-Nevada Academy of Science*, Vol. 15, pp. 19.

Lokeshwari, and Chandrappa (2006), "Impact of heavy metal contamination of Bellandur Lake on soil and cultivated Vegetation", *Current science*, Vol. 91, No. 5, pp. 622-627.

Maurice, C, A. Bergman, H. Ecke and A. Lagerkvist (1995), "Vegetation as a biological indicator for landfill gas emissions. Initial investigations". *Proceedings of Sardinia '95, Fifth International Landfill symposium, S. Margherita di Pula, Italy,*

Melesse, Assefa M, Nangia Vijay, Wang Xixi and McClain Michael (2007), "Wetland Restoration Response Analysis using MODIS and Groundwater Data". *Sensors.* 7, pp. 1916-1933.

Menon, Ajit (2004), "Colonial constructions of agrarian fields and forests in the Kolli Hills", *Indian Economic and Social History Review*, Vol. 41, No. 3., pp. 14-337

Millennium Ecosystem Assessment (2005), "Ecosystems and human well-being: Wetlands and Water Synthesis", *World Resources Institute*, Washington DC.

Mitchell, R. C and R. T. Carson (1989), "Using Surveys to Value Public Goods: the Contingent Valuation Method", *Resources for the Future*, Washington, D. C.

Mitsch, William. Jand James G. Gosselink (1993), "Wetlands" VanNostrand Reinhold, New York. 2nd Edition.

Mitsch, William. JandJamesG. Gosselink (2000), "Special issue the values of wetlands: landscapes and institutional perspectives: The value of wetlands: importance of scale and landscape Setting", *Ecological Economics*, Vol. 35, No. 200, pp. 25–33.

Mitsch, William. J. and S. E. Jorgensen (2004), "Ecological Engineering and Ecosystem Restoration". *John Wiley & Sons, Inc.*, New York. pp. 411.

Nagendran, R, A. Selvam and Kurian Joseph (2007), "Effect of Municipal Solid Waste on Floral Diversity and Plant Growth – A Case Study at Perungudi and Kodungaiyur Dumping Grounds, Chennai, India", Centre for Environmental Studies, Anna University, Chennai, India co-ordinated by Asian Institute of Technology, Thailand, pp. 1-16.

National Wetland Atlas (2011), Sponsored by Ministry of Environment and Forests, Government of India; National Wetland Inventory and Assessment (NWIA), Space Applications Centre (ISRO), Ahmedabad.

NEERI (1999), "Review of Environmental Impact Assessment of Pallikaranai Development Area, Chennai", National Environmental Engineering Research Institute (NEERI), Nagpur, India.

Nixon, S. W. and V. Lec (1986) " Wetlands and Water Quality", Wetlands Res. Prog. Tech. ReP, Y-86-2, Water Way Exp, US Army Eng.

Padmavathi, M (2008), "Assessment of Ground Contamination at Perungudi Municipal Dumping Yard in Chennai". The 12th International Conference of International Association for Computer Methods and Advances in Geomechanics (*IACMAG*),1-6 October, 2008 Goa, India.

Pandey, J. S, V. Joseph and S. N. Kaul (2004), A Zone-Wise Ecological-Economic Analysis of Indian Wetlands, *Environmental Monitoring and Assessment*, Vol. 98, pp. 261–273.

Panigrahi, S and Acharya. B (2007), "Anthropogenic Impact on Water Quality of Chilika Lagoon RAMSAR site-A Statistical Approach", *Wetlands Ecol Management*, Vol. 15, pp. 113–126.

Patnaik, Dipankar. C and Srihari Priya (2004), "Wetlands - A development paradox: The dilemma of South Chennai, India". *Social Science Research Network (SSRN)*. September 19, 2004.

Pauchard, A, M. Aguayo, E. Pena, R. Urrutia (2006), "Multiple effects of urbanization on the biodiversity of developing countries: The case of a fast-growing metropolitan area (Concepción, Chile)", *Biological Conservation*, Vol. 127, No. 3, pp. 272-28.

Portney, PR (1994), "The contingent valuation debate: why economists should care", *Journal of Economic Perspectives*, Vol. 8, pp. 3– 17.

Prabu (2009), "Impact of Heavy Metal Contamination of Akaki River of Ethiopia on Soil and Metal Toxicity on Cultivated Vegetable Crops", *Electronic Journal of Industrial agricultural and Food Chemistry*, Vol. 8, pp. 818-827.

Prasad, G and Narayana. S (2007), "Spatial distribution of Pollution Parameters and Suitability of Groundwater for Irrigation in Sarda River Basin, South India", *Journal of IPHE*, No. 4, pp. 33-38.

Raj, P. P. N, J. Ranjini, R. Dhanya, J. Subramanian, P. A. Azeez and S. Bhupathy (2010), "Consolidated checklist of birds in the Pallikaranai Wetlands, Chennai, India", *Journal of Threatened Taxa*, Vol. 2. No. 8, pp 1114-1118.

Raman and Narayanan. S (2008), "Impact of solild waste effect on ground water and soil quality nearer to pallavaram solid waste landfill site in Chennai", *Rasayan Journal of Chemistry*, Vol. 11, pp. 828-836.

Romshoo, Shakil Ahmad, Ali Nahida and Rashid Irfan (2011), "Geoinformatics for characterizing and understanding the spatio-temporal dynamics (1969 to 2008) of Hokersar wetland in Kashmir Himalayas", *International Journal of the Physical Sciences* Vol. 6, No. 5, pp. 1026-1038.

Sarkar, Jaimini (2011), "Ramsar Convention and India", *Current Science*, Vol. 101, No. 10, pp. 1266-1268.

Sawhney, A (2006), "An evaluation of domestic and trade policies in building environmental services capacity in Asia: Balancing diverse interests and priorities", In: Delivering Sustainable Development in Negotiations on Environmental Goods and Services, Geneva, Switzerland.

Scott, D. A and T. A. Jones (1995), "Classification and Inventory of wetlands: A global over review", *Vegetation*, Vol. 118, pp. 3-16.

Tessier, A, P. G. C. Campbell and M. Bisson (1979), "Sequential extraction procedure for the speciation of particulate trace metals". *Analytical Chemistry*, Vol. 51, pp. 844– 851.

Turner, Kerry R, J. M. Jeroen van den Bergh, Tore So derqvist, Aat Barendregt, Jan van der Straaten, Edward Maltby and EkkoVan Ierland (2000), "Ecological-economic analysis of wetlands: scientific integration for management and policy", Special Issue the Values of Wetlands: Landscape and Institutional Perspectives, *Ecological Economics*, Vol. 35, pp. 7–23.

Turner, K, J. Paavola, P. Cooper, S. Farber, V. JessamyandS. Georgiou (2003), "Valuing nature:lessons learned and future research directions", *Ecological Economics*, Vol. 46, pp. 493-510.

Turner, Kerry R, Georgiou, Stavros, Brouwer, Roy, Bateman, J. Ian and I. J. Langford (2003), "Towards an Integrated Environmental Assessment for Wetland and Catchment Management", *The Geographical Journal*, Vol. 33, pp. 99-116.

UNEP, 1994, "Pollution of lakes and rivers". *UNEP Environmental Library* No:12, Nairobi, Kenya.

Vasanthi, P, S. Kaliappan and R. Srinivasaraghavan (2008). "Impact of poor solid waste management on ground water", *Environ Monit Assess*, Vol. 143, pp. 227–238

Vencatesan, Jayshree (2007), "Protecting wetlands", *Current Science*, Vol. 93, No. 3, pp. 288-290.

Venkatachalam, L (2004), "Designing Contingent Valuation (CV) Surveys for Estimating Use Values: Some Experience from a Case Study of a Water Supply Project", *Journal of Social and Economic Development*, Vol. 5, No. 2, pp. 267 – 284.

Vijayan, V. S, S. N. Prasad, L. Vijayan and S. Muralidharan (2004), "Inland Wetlands of India – Conservation Priorities ", Sálim Ali Centre for Ornithology & Natural History, Coimbatore. pp. xxiv + 532.

Walsh, RG, J. B. Loomis and R. A. Gillman (1984), "Valuing option, existence and bequest demands for wilderness", *Land Economics*, Vol. 60, pp. 14 – 29.

Wanga, Wei and Hea Wenshan (2007), "Ecosystem service values and restoration in the urban Sanyang wetland of Wenzhou, China", *Ecological Engineering*. 29, pp. 249–258

Whittington, Dale (1998), "Administering Contingent Valuation Surveys in Developing Countries", *World Development*, Vol. 26, No. 1, pp. 21-30.

WHO, (1984), "Guidelines for drinking water qudlity" V. 1 Recommendations, World Health Organization, Geneva 27, Switzerland, pp. 130.

WHO,(1994), "Declaration on occupational health for all", *World Health Organization Avenue Appia* 20, 1211, World Health Organization, Geneva 27, Switzerland.

WHO, (1999), Guideline for drinking water quality, 2nd ed., Health criteria and other supporting information, World Health Organization, Geneva 27, Switzerland

World Bank (1992), World Development Report, *Development and the Environment, World Bank, Washington DC,*.